FIRST AND LAST THINGS

VOLUMES PUBLISHED IN THE SERIES.

The Thinker's Library, No. 1.

FIRST AND LAST THINGS

A CONFESSION OF FAITH AND RULE OF LIFE

BY

H. G. WELLS

THE DEFINITIVE EDITION

LONDON:

WATTS & CO.,

5 and 6 JOHNSON'S COURT, FLEET STREET, E.C.4

It should be clearly understood that each writer in this series of little books is alone responsible for the opinions expressed.

First published in the Thinker's Library, February, 1929.
Second Impression, July, 1930.

Printed and Published in Great Britain for the Rationalist Press
Association Limited by Watts & Co. (C. A. Watts & Co.
Limited), 5 & 6 Johnson's Court, Fleet Street, London, E.C.4.

CONTENTS

BOOK I

METAPHYSICS

BOOK II

OF BELIEFS

BOOK III

OF GENERAL CONDUCT

CONTENTS

BOOK IV

SOME PERSONAL THINGS

BOOK THE FIRST

METAPHYSICS

§ I

THE NECESSITY FOR METAPHYSICS

As a preliminary to that experiment in mutual confession from which this book arose, I found it necessary to consider and state certain truths about the nature of knowledge, about the meaning of truth and the value of words, that is to say I found I had to begin by being metaphysical. In writing out these notes now I think it is well that I should state just how important I think this metaphysical prelude is.

There is a popular prejudice against metaphysics as something at once difficult and fruitless, as an idle system of inquiries remote from any human interest. As a matter of fact metaphysical inquiries are a necessary condition to all clear thinking. I suppose this odd misconception arose from the vulgar pretensions of pedants, from their appeal to ancient names and their quotations in unfamiliar tongues, and from the easy fall into technicality of men struggling to be explicit where a high degree of explicitness is impossible. Metaphysics is a discussion of our general ideas, and naturally therefore intelligent metaphysical discussion is hardly possible except in the mother tongue in which those general ideas arose in our minds. But the interests and the pedantries that control higher education in Britain, and influence it very powerfully in America, have

imposed upon the proper study and teaching of metaphysics the absurd condition that it should be studied
in connection with the badly-taught and little known
language of Ancient Greece.   So a naturally elementary discussion has been made into an intricate and
allusive one.   It needs erudition and accumulated
and alien literature to make metaphysics obscure,
and some of the most fruitful and able metaphysical
discussion in the world was conducted by a number
of unhampered men in small Greek cities, who knew
no language but their own and had scarcely a tech-
nical term.   The true metaphysician is after all only
a person who says, " Now let us take thought for a
moment before we fall into a discussion of the broad
questions of life, lest we rush hastily into impossible
and needless conflict.   What is the exact value of
these thoughts we are thinking and these words we
are using ? " He wants to take thought about thought.
There are, of course, ardent spirits who, on the con-
trary, want to plunge into action or controversy or
belief without taking thought ; they feel that there is
not time to examine thought.   " While you argue,"
they say, " the house is burning."   They are the kin
of those who rush and struggle and make panics in
theatre fires.   But they are not likely to be among
the readers of this book.

It seems to me that most of the troubles of humanity are really misunderstandings.   Men's compositions
and characters are, I think, more similar than their
views, and if they had not needlessly different modes
of expression upon many broad issues, they would be
practically at one upon a hundred matters where now
they widely differ.

Most of the great controversies of the world, most
of the wide religious differences that keep men apart,
arise from this : from differences in their way of
thinking.   Men imagine they stand on the same

ground and mean the same thing by the same words,
whereas they stand on slightly different grounds, use
different terms for the same thing and express the
same thing in different words. Logomachies, conflict
about words—into such death-traps of effort do
ardent spirits run and perish.

This has been said before by numberless people.
It has been said before by numberless people, but it
seems to me it has been realized by very few—and
until it is realized to the fullest extent, we shall
continue to live at intellectual cross-purposes and
waste the forces of our species needlessly and abundantly.

This persuasion is a very important thing in my
mind.

I think that the time has come when the modern
mind must take up metaphysical discussion again—
when it must resume those subtle but necessary and
unavoidable problems which have been so markedly
shirked for many years, when it must get to a common and general understanding upon what its ideas
of truth, good, and beauty amount to, and upon the
relation of the name to the thing, and of the relation
of one mind to another mind in the matter of resemblance and the matter of difference—upon all those
issues the young science student is apt to dismiss as
Rot, and the young classical student as Gas, and the
austere student of the science of Economics as Theo-
rizing, unsuitable for his methods of research.

In our achievement of understandings in the place
of these evasions about fundamental things lies the
road, I believe, along which the human mind can
escape, if ever it is to escape, from the confusion of
purposes that distracts it at the present time.

§ 2

CURRENT METAPHYSICAL TEACHING ABSURD

When the intellectual history of our time comes to be written I think that nothing will more impress the students of these years than the extraordinary evasion of metaphysical enlightenment in the education of our youth.   Here were exercises and disciplines essential to the proper development of any good mind ; here were questions intensely attractive to any intelligent youth ; here were the common tests and filters for all knowledge and decision, and the youth of the big English-speaking community was almost deliberately kept away from and cheated out of this strengthening gymnastic.   No wonder that the English-speaking mind had an understanding like a broken sieve and a will as capable of definite forms as a dropped egg.   Philosophical study, the common material for every type of sound adolescent education, was stuck away into remote pretentious courses, behind barriers of Greek linguistic training, as if it were something too high for normal minds, too mystical for current speech.   A general need was treated as a precious luxury.   At Oxford instead of calling the philosophical course " Elements," the future historian will remark, with derision, they called it " Greats."

And when this student of things intellectual has done with the general preposterousness of a huge modern community treating philosophy as a remote special subject reserved for a small minority of university students, he will find still more matter for amazement and laughter in our way of teaching philosophy.   We do not bring the young mind up against the few broad elemental questions that are *the questions of metaphysics*, the questions that provide *the* basis of all clear thinking.   We do not make it discuss, correct it, elucidate it. That was the way of the Greeks, and we worship that divine people far too much to adopt their way. No, we lecture to our young people about not philosophy but philosophers, we put them through book after book, telling how other people have discussed these questions. We avoid the questions of metaphysics, but we deliver semi-digested half-views of the discussions of, and answers to, these questions made by men of all sorts and qualities, in various remote languages and under conditions quite different from our own. In their histories the essential questions are presently completely lost sight of. We give them compact (and indeed highly desiccated) accounts of the philosophy of Aristotle, Plato, Hegel, Locke, Descartes, and so on and so on. It is as if we began teaching arithmetic by long lectures upon the origin of the Roman numerals and then went on to the lives and motives of the Arab mathematicians in Spain, or started with Roger Bacon in chemistry or Sir Richard Owen in comparative anatomy. A little while ago I had a most edifying conversation with two young women who had been " doing " and who had " done," bless them ! " philosophy " in the Universities of London and Cambridge respectively. They had shared experiences of a lecturer, I forget his name, who lectures in both these radiant centres of wisdom. This incredible person lectures, they assured me, upon all philosophies ancient and modern. Poor Omniscience just knows everything, but this marvel knows what everybody has thought about everything. He told his classes what they all thought, all these wise men, and how they " derived " one from another. These two young people were in consequence more like bags of broken fragments from the ages than living intelligences ; they discussed glibly of the Platonic Ideal and the Golden Mean, of Categories and Impera-

tives, of Induction and Syllogism and Materialism ;
if you spoke of Plotinus they whispered " Mysticism,"
and if you said Lucretius, the atoms glittered in their
eyes.   Also they had a fine stock of lecture-room anec-
dotes.   I tried them then upon one or two current
questions.   And on the whole they thought rather
worse than if they had spent these same studious
years upon embroidery.

It is time the educational powers began to realize
that the questions of metaphysics, the elements of
philosophy, are, here and now, to be done afresh in
each mind.   So far as the thought that has gone
before us enlightens our present inquiry, so far it lives
still.   The rest is for the museum and the special
scholar.   What is wanted is philosophy, and not a
shallow smattering of the history of philosophy.   Our
children ask for bread and we give them worn mill-
stones. . . .

The proper way to discuss metaphysics, like the
proper way to discuss mathematics or chemistry, is
to discuss the accumulated and digested product of
human thought in such matters.   Only in creative
literature and because of beauty are texts immortal.
The reverence for texts and the " systems " of individuals in the case of philosophy is just as absurd
and mischievous as it would be in the case of science.
The only philosophy that a man is entitled to ex-
pound and discuss is that which he has made his own.
I make no apology therefore in annexing every philosophical idea and phrase from the past that I have
cared to assimilate.   This is *my* system that I place
before you in order that you should make *your* system.   You can no more think about the world according to another man's system than you can look at it
with a dead man's eye.

§ 3

THE WORLD OF FACT

Necessarily, when one begins an inquiry into the fundamental nature of oneself and one's mind and its processes, one is forced into biography. I begin by asking how the conscious mind with which I identify myself began.

It presents itself to me as a history of a perception of a world of facts opening out from an accidental centre at which I happened to begin.

I do not attempt to define this word fact. Fact expresses for me something in its nature primary and unanalysable. I start from that. I take as a typical statement of fact that I sit here at my desk writing with a fountain-pen on a pad of ruled scribbling paper, that the sunlight falls upon me and throws the shadow of the window mullion across the page, that Peter, my cat, sleeps on the window-seat close at hand, and that this agate paper-weight with the silver top that once was Henley's holds my loose memoranda together. Outside is a patch of lawn and then a fringe of winter-bitten iris leaves and then the sea, greatly wrinkled and astir under the south-west wind. There is a boat going out which I think may be Jim Pain's, but of that I cannot be sure. . . .

These are statements of a certain quality, a quality that extends through a huge universe in which I find myself placed.

I try to recall how this world of fact arose in my mind. It began with a succession of limited immediate scenes and of certain minutely perceived persons ; I recall an underground kitchen with a drawered table, a window looking up at a grating, a back-yard in which, growing out by a dust-bin, was a grape-vine ; a red-papered room with a bookcase, over my father's shop, the dusty aisles and fixtures, the regiments of wine-glasses and tumblers, the rows of hanging mugs and jugs, the towering edifices of jam-pots, the tea and dinner and toilet sets in that emporium, its brighter side of cricket goods, of pads and balls and stumps. Out of the window one peeped at the more exterior world, the High Street in front, the tailor's garden, the butcher's yard, the churchyard, and Bromley church tower behind ; and one was taken upon expeditions to fields and open places. This limited world was peopled with certain familiar presences, mother and father, two brothers, the evasive but interesting cat, and by intermittent people of a livelier but more transient interest, customers and callers.

Such was my opening world of fact, and each day it enlarged and widened and had more things added to it. I had soon won my way to speech and was hearing of facts beyond my visible world of fact. Presently I was at a Dame's school and learning to read.

From the centre of that little world as primary, as the initiatory material, my perception of the world of fact widened and widened, by new sights and sounds, by reading and hearing descriptions and histories, by guesses and inferences ; my curiosity and interest, my appetite for fact, grew by what it fed upon, I carried on my expansion of the world of fact until it took me through the mineral and fossil galleries of the Natural History Museum, through the geological drawers of the College of Science, through a year of dissection and some weeks at the astronomical telescope. So I built up my conceptions of a real world out of facts observed and out of inferences of a nature akin to fact, of a world immense and enduring receding interminably into space and time. In that I found myself placed, a creature relatively infinitesimal, needing and struggling. It was clear to me, by a hundred considerations, that I in my body upon this planet Earth, was the outcome of countless generations of conflict and begetting, the creature of natural selection, the heir of good and bad engendered in that struggle.

So my world of fact shaped itself. I find it altogether impossible to question or doubt that world of fact. Particular facts one may question as facts. For instance, I think I see an unseasonable yellow wallflower from my windows, but you may dispute that and show it is only a broken end of iris leaf accidentally lit to yellow. That is merely a substitution of fact for fact. One may doubt whether one is perceiving or remembering or telling facts clearly, but the persuasion that there are facts independent of one's interpretations and obdurate to one's will remains invincible.

§ 4

SCEPTICISM OF THE INSTRUMENT

At first I took the world of fact as being exactly as I perceived it. I believed my eyes. Seeing was believing, I thought. Still more did I believe my reasoning. It was only slowly that I began to suspect that the world of fact could be anything different from the clear picture it made upon my mind.

I realized the inadequacy of the senses first. Into that I will not enter here. Any proper textbook of physiology or psychology will supply a number of instances of the habitual deceptions of sight and touch and hearing. I came upon these things in my reading, in the laboratory, with microscope or telescope, lived with them as constant difficulties. I will only instance one trifling case of visual deception in order to lead to my next question. One draws two lines strictly parallel ; so

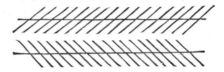

Oblique to them one draws a series of lines ; so

and instantly the parallelism seems to be disturbed. If the second figure is presented to any one without sufficient science to understand this delusion, the impression is created that these lines converge to the right and diverge to the left. The vision is deceived in its mental factor, and judges wrongly of the thing seen.

In this case we are able to measure the distance of the lines, to find how the main lines looked before the cross ones were drawn, to bring the deception up against fact of a different sort and so correct the mistake. If the ignorant observer were unable to do that, he might remain permanently under the impression that the main lines were out of parallelism. And all the infirmities of eye and ear, touch and taste, are discovered and checked by the fact that the erroneous impressions presently strike against fact and discover an incompatibility with it. If they did not we should never have discovered them. If on the other hand they are so incompatible with fact as to endanger the lives of the beings labouring under such infirmities, they would tend to be eliminated from among our defects.

The presumption to which biological science brings one is that the senses and mind will work as well as the survival of the species may require, but that they will not work so very much better. There is no ground in matter-of-fact experience for assuming that there is any more inevitable certitude about purely intellectual operations than there is about sensory perceptions. The mind of a man may be primarily only a food-seeking, danger-avoiding, mate-finding instrument, just as the mind of a dog is, just as the nose of a dog is, or the snout of a pig.

You see the strong preparatory reason there is in this view of life for entertaining the suppositions that—

The senses seem surer than they are.

The thinking mind seems clearer than it is and is more positive than it ought to be.

The world of fact is not what it appears to be.

These preliminary assumptions were already strongly established in my mind before I began to philosophize at all.

§ 5

THE CLASSIFICATORY ASSUMPTION

After I had studied science, and particularly biological science, for some years, I became a teacher in a school for boys. I found it necessary to supplement my untutored conception of teaching method by a more systematic knowledge of its principles and methods, and I took the courses for the diplomas of Licentiate and Fellow of the London College of Preceptors which happened to be convenient for me. These courses included some of the more elementary

aspects of psychology and logic and set me thinking
and reading further.   From the first, Logic as it was
presented to me impressed me as a system of ideas
and methods remote and secluded from the world of
fact in which I lived and with which I had to deal.
As it came to me in the ordinary textbooks, it presented itself as the science of inference using the syllogism as its principal instrument.   Now I was first
struck by the fact that while my teachers in Logic
seemed to be assuring me I always thought in this
form :—

> " M is P.
> S is M.
> S is P. "

the method of my reasoning was almost always in
this form :—

> " S_1 is more or less P.
> S_2 is very similar to S_1.
> S_2 is very probably but not certainly more or less P.
> Let us go on that assumption and see how it works."

That is to say, I was constantly reasoning by analogy and applying verification.   So far from using the
syllogistic form confidently, I habitually distrusted
it as anything more than a test of consistency in
statement.   But I found the textbooks of logic disposed to ignore my customary method of reasoning
altogether or to recognize it only where S_1 and S_2
could be lumped together under a common name.
Then they put it something after this form as Induction :—

> " S_1, S_2, S_3, and S_4 are P.
> $S_1 + S_2 + S_3 + S_4 + \ldots$ are all S.
> All S is P."

I looked into the laws of thought and into the
postulates upon which the syllogistic logic is based,

and it slowly became clear to me that from my point of view, the point of view of one who seeks truth and reality, logic assumed a belief in the objective reality of classification of which my studies in biology and mineralogy had largely disabused me. Logic, it seemed to me, had taken a common innate error of the mind and had emphasized it in order to develop a system of reasoning that should be exact in its processes. I turned my attention to the examination of that. For in common with the general run of illiterate men I had supposed that logic professed to supply a trustworthy science and method for the investigation and expression of reality.

A mind nourished on anatomical study is of course permeated with the suggestion of the vagueness and instability of biological species. A biological species is quite obviously a great number of unique individuals which is separable from other biological species only by the fact that an enormous number of other linking individuals are inaccessible in time—are in other words dead and gone—and each new individual in that species does, in the distinction of its own individuality, break away in however infinitesimal degree from the previous average properties of the species. There is no property of any species, even the properties that constitute the specific definition, that is not a matter of more or less.

If, for example, a species be distinguished by a single large red spot on the back, you will find if you go over a great number of specimens that red spot shrinking here to nothing, expanding there to a more general redness, weakening to pink, deepening to russet and brown, shading into crimson, and so on and so on. And this is true not only of biological species. It is true of the mineral specimens constituting a mineral species, and I remember as a constant refrain in the lectures of Professor Judd upon rock classification, the words, "they pass into one another by insensible gradations." It is true, I hold, of all things.

You will think perhaps of atoms of the elements as instances of identically similar things, but these are things not of experience but of theory, and there is not a phenomenon in chemistry that is not equally well explained on the supposition that it is merely the immense quantities of atoms necessarily taken in any experiment that marks by the operation of the law of averages the fact that each atom also has its unique quality, its special individual difference.

This ideal of uniqueness in all individuals is not only true of the classifications of material science; it is true and still more evidently true of the species of common thought; it is true of common terms. Take the word *Chair*. When one says chair, one thinks vaguely of an average chair. But collect individual instances; think of arm-chairs and reading-chairs and dining-room chairs, and kitchen chairs, chairs that pass into benches, chairs that cross the boundary and become settees, dentists' chairs, thrones, opera stalls, seats of all sorts, those miraculous fungoid growths that cumber the floor of the Arts and Crafts Exhibition, and you will perceive what a lax bundle in fact is this simple straightforward term. In co-operation with an intelligent joiner I would undertake to defeat any definition of chair or chairishness that you gave me. Chairs just as much as individual organisms, just as much as mineral and rock specimens, are unique things—if you know them well enough you will find an individual difference even in a set of machine-made chairs—and it is only because we do not possess minds of unlimited capacity, because our brain has only a limited number of pigeon-holes for our correspondence with an unlimited universe of objective uniques, that we have to delude ourselves into the belief that there is a chairishness in this species common to and distinctive of all chairs.

Classification and number, which in truth ignore the fine differences of objective realities, have in the past of human thought been imposed upon things. . . .

Greek thought impresses me as being over-much obsessed by an objective treatment of certain necessary preliminary conditions of human thought—number and definition and class and abstract form! But these things—number, definition, class and abstract form—I hold, are merely unavoidable conditions of mental activity—regrettable conditions rather than essential facts. *The forceps of our minds are clumsy forceps and crush the truth a little in taking hold of it.* . . .

Let me give you a rough figure of what I am trying to convey in this first attack upon the philosophical validity of general terms. You have seen the result of those various methods of black-and-white reproduction that involve the use of a rectangular net. You know the sort of process picture I mean—it used to be employed very frequently in reproducing photographs. At a little distance you really seem to have a faithful reproduction of the original picture, but when you peer closely you find not the unique form and masses of the original, but a multitude of little rectangles, uniform in shape and size. The more earnestly you go into the thing, the closelier you look, the more the picture is lost in reticulations. I submit, the world of reasoned inquiry has a very similar relation to the world of fact. For the rough purposes of every day the network picture will do, but the finer your purpose the less it will serve, and for an ideally fine purpose, for absolute and general knowledge that will be as true for a man at a distance with a telescope as for a man with a microscope, it will not serve at all.

It is true you can make your net of logical interpretations finer and finer, you can fine your classification more and more—up to a certain limit. But
essentially you are working in limits, and as you
come closer, as you look at finer and subtler things,
as you leave the practical purpose for which the
method exists, the element of error increases. Every
species is vague, every term goes cloudy at its edges ;
and so, in my way of thinking, relentless logic is only
another name for a stupidity—for a sort of intellectual pigheadedness. If you push a philosophical or
metaphysical inquiry through a series of valid syllo-
gisms—never committing any generally recognized
fallacy—you nevertheless leave behind you at each
step a certain rubbing and marginal loss of objective
truth, and you get deflections that are difficult to
trace at each phase in the process. Every species
waggles about in its definition, every tool is a little
loose in its handle, every scale has its individual
error. So long as you are reasoning for practical purposes about finite things of experience, you can every
now and then check your process and correct your
adjustments. But not when you make what are
called philosophical and theological inquiries, when
you turn your implement towards the final absolute
truth of things.

This real vagueness of class terms is equally true
whether we consider those terms used extensively or
intensively, that is to say whether in relation to all
the members of the species or in relation to an imaginary typical specimen. The logician begins by de-
claring that S is either pink or not pink. In the world
of fact it is the rarest thing to encounter this absolute
alternative ; S_1 is pink, but S_2 is pinker, S_3 is scarcely
pink at all, and one is in doubt whether S_4 is not
properly to be called scarlet. The finest type specimen you can find simply has the characteristic qual-

ity a little more rather than a little less. The neat little circles the logician uses to convey his idea of pink or not pink to the student are just pictures of boundaries in his mind, exaggerations of a natural mental tendency. They are required for the purposes of his science, but they are departures from the nature of fact.

§ 6

EMPTY TERMS

Classes in logic are not only represented by circles with a hard firm outline, whereas in fact they have no such definite limits, but also there is a constant disposition to think of all names as if they represented positive classes. With words just as with numbers and abstract forms there have been definite phases of human development. There was, with regard to number, the phase when man could barely count at all, or counted in perfect good faith and sanity upon his fingers. Then there was the phase when he struggled with the development of number, when he began to elaborate all sorts of ideas about numbers, until at last he developed complex superstitions about perfect numbers and imperfect numbers, about threes and sevens and the like. The same was the case with abstract forms; and even to-day we are scarcely more than heads out of the vast subtle muddle of thinking about spheres and ideally perfect forms and so on, that was the price of this little necessary step to clear thinking. How large a part numerical and geometric magic, numerical and geometrical philosophy, have played in the history of the mind! And the whole apparatus of language and mental communication is beset with like dangers. The language of the elemental savage is, I suppose, purely positive ; the thing has a name, the name has a thing.   This indeed is the tradition of language, and even to-day we, when we hear a name, are predisposed—and sometimes it is a very vicious disposition—to imagine forthwith something answering to the name.   *We are disposed, as an incurable mental vice, to accumulate intension in terms.*   If I say to you Wodget or Crump, you find yourself passing over the fact that these are nothings ; these are, so to speak, mere blankety blanks, and trying to think what sort of thing a Wodget or a Crump may be.   You find yourself led insensibly by subtle associations of sound and ideas to giving these blank terms attributes.

Now, this is true not only of quite empty terms, but of terms that carry a meaning.   It is a mental necessity that we should make classes and use general terms, and as soon as we do that we fall into immediate danger of unjustifiably increasing the intension of these terms.   You will find a large proportion of human prejudice and misunderstanding arises from this universal proclivity.

§ 7

NEGATIVE TERMS

There is a particular sort of empty terms that has been and is conspicuously dangerous to the thinker, the class of negative terms.   The negative term is in plain fact just nothing ; " Not-A " is the absence of any trace of the quality that constitutes A, it is the rest of everything for ever.   But there seems to be a real bias in the mind towards regarding " Not-A " as a thing mysteriously in the nature of A, as though " Not-A " and A were species of the same genus. When one speaks of Not-Pink one is apt to think of green things and yellow things and to ignore anger

or abstract nouns or the sound of thunder. And
logicians, following the normal bias of the mind, do
actually present A and Not-A in this sort of dia-
gram :—

ignoring altogether the difficult case of the space in
which these words are printed. Obviously the dia-
gram that comes nearer experienced fact is :—

Not Ⓐ A

with no outer boundary. But the logician finds it
necessary for his processes [1] to present that outer
Not-A as bounded, and so speak of the total area of
A and Not-A as the Universe of Discourse ; and the
metaphysician and the common-sense thinker alike
fall far too readily into the belief that this convention of method is an adequate representation of fact.

Let me try and express how in my mind this matter of negative terms has shaped itself. I think of
something which I may perhaps best describe as
being off the stage or out of court, or as the Void
without Implications, or as Nothingness, or as Outer
Darkness. This is a sort of hypothetical Beyond to
the visible world of human thought, and thither I
think all negative terms reach at last, and merge, and
become nothing. Whatever positive class you make,
whatever boundary you draw, straight away from
that boundary begins the corresponding negative

---

[1] *Vide* e.g. Keyne's *Formal Logic re* Euler's diagrams and
Immediate Inferences.

class and passes into the illimitable horizon of nothingness. You talk of pink things; you ignore, as the
arbitrary postulates of Logic direct, the more elusive
shades of pink, and draw your line. Beyond is the
not-pink, known and knowable, and still in the not-
pink region one comes to the Outer Darkness. Not
blue, not happy, not iron, all the *not* classes meet in
that Outer Darkness. That same Outer Darkness
and nothingness is infinite space and infinite time
and any being of infinite qualities; and all that region
I rule out of court in my philosophy altogether. I
will neither affirm nor deny if I can help it about
any *not* things. I will not deal with *not* things at all,
except by accident and inadvertence. If I use the
word "infinite" I use it as one often uses "countless," "the countless hosts of the enemy"—or "immeasurable"—"immeasurable cliffs"—that is to
say, as the limit of measurement, as a convenient
equivalent to as many times this cloth yard as you
can, and as many again, and so on and so on until
you and your numerical system are beaten to a
standstill.

Now, a great number of apparently positive terms
are, or have become, practically negative terms and
are under the same ban with me. A considerable
number of terms that have played a great part in the
world of thought seem to me to be invalidated by
this same defect, to have no content or an undefined
content or an unjustifiable content. For example,
that word Omniscient, as implying infinite knowledge, impresses me as being a word with a delusive
air of being solid and full, when it is really hollow
with no content whatever. I am persuaded that
knowing is the relation of a conscious being to something not itself, that the thing known is defined as a
system of parts and aspects and relationships, that
knowledge is comprehension, and so that only finite

things can know or be known. When you talk of a being of infinite extension and infinite duration, omniscient and omnipotent and perfect, you seem to me to be talking in negatives of nothing whatever.

§ 8

LOGIC STATIC AND LIFE KINETIC

Not only are class terms vague with regard to these marginal instances, but they are also vague in time. The current syllogistic logic rests on the assumption that either A is B or it is not B. The practical reality is that nothing is permanent ; A is always becoming more or less B or ceasing to be more or less B. But it would seem the human mind cannot manage with that. It has to hold a thing still for a moment before it can think it. It arrests the present moment for its struggle as Joshua stopped the sun. It cannot contemplate things continuously, and so it has to resort to a series of static snapshots. It has to kill motion in order to study it, as a naturalist kills and pins out a butterfly in order to study life.

You see the mind is really pigeon-holed and discontinuous in two respects, in respect to time and in respect to classification ; whereas one has a strong persuasion that the world of fact is unbounded or continuous.

§ 9

PLANES AND DIALECTS OF THOUGHT

Finally : the Logician, intent upon perfecting the certitudes of his methods rather than upon expressing the confusing subtleties of truth, has done little to help thinking men in the perpetual difficulty that arises from the fact that the universe can be seen in many different fashions and expressed by many different systems of terms, each expression within its limits true and yet incommensurable with expression upon a differing system. There is a sort of stratification in human ideas. I have it very much in mind that various terms in our reasoning lie, as it were, at different levels and in different planes, and that we accomplish a large amount of error and confusion by reasoning terms together that do not lie or nearly lie in the same plane.

Let me endeavour to make myself a little less obscure by a flagrant instance from physical things. Suppose some one began to talk seriously of a man seeing an atom through a microscope, or better perhaps of cutting one in half with a knife. There are a number of non-analytical people who would be quite prepared to believe that an atom could be visible to the eye or cut in this manner. But any one at all conversant with physical conceptions would almost as soon think of killing the square root of 2 with a rook rifle as of cutting an atom in half with a knife. One's conception of an atom is reached through a process of hypothesis and analysis, and in the world of atoms there are no knives and no men to cut. If you have thought with a strong consistent mental movement, then, when you have thought of your atom under the knife blade, your knife blade has itself become a cloud of swinging grouped atoms, and your microscope lens a little universe of oscillatory and vibratory molecules. If you think of the universe, thinking at the level of atoms, there is neither knife to cut, scale to weigh, nor eye to see. The universe at that plane to which the mind of the molecular physicist descends has none of the shapes or forms of our common life whatever. This hand with which I write is, in the universe of molecular physics, a cloud of warring atoms and molecules, combining and recombining, colliding, rotating, flying hither and thither in the universal atmosphere of ether.

You see, I hope, what I mean when I say that the universe of molecular physics is at a different level from the universe of common experience;—what we call stable and solid is in that world a freely moving system of interlacing centres of force, what we call colour and sound is there no more than this length of vibration or that. We have reached to a conception of that universe of molecular physics by a great enterprise of organized analysis, and our universe of daily experiences stands in relation to that elemental world as if it were a synthesis of those elemental things.

I would suggest to you that this is only a very extreme instance of the general state of affairs, that there may be finer and subtler differences of level between one term and another, and that terms may very well be thought of as lying obliquely and as being twisted through different levels.

It will perhaps give a clearer idea of what I am seeking to convey if I suggest a concrete image for the whole world of a man's thought and knowledge. Imagine a large clear jelly, in which at all angles and in all states of simplicity or contortion his ideas are embedded. They are all valid and possible ideas as they lie, none incompatible with any. If you imagine the direction of up or down in this clear jelly being as it were the direction in which one moves by analysis or by synthesis, if you go down, for example, from matter to atoms and centres of force and up to men and states and countries—if you will imagine the ideas lying in that manner—you will get the beginnings of my intention. But our instrument, our process of thinking, like a drawing before the discovery of perspective, appears to have difficulties with the third dimension, appears capable only of dealing with or reasoning about ideas by projecting them upon the same plane. It will be obvious that a great multitude of things may very well exist together in a solid jelly, which would be overlapping and incompatible and mutually destructive when projected together upon one plane. Through the bias in our instrument to do this, through reasoning between terms not in the same plane, an enormous amount of confusion, perplexity and mental deadlocking occurs.

The old theological deadlock between predestination and free will serves admirably as an example of the sort of deadlock I mean. Take life at the level of common sensation and common experience and there is no more indisputable fact than man's freedom of will, unless it is his complete moral responsibility. But make only the least penetrating of scientific analyses and you perceive a world of inevitable consequences, a rigid succession of cause and effect. Insist upon a flat agreement between the two, and there you are! The instrument fails.

So far as this particular opposition is concerned, I shall point out later the reasonableness and convenience of regarding the common-sense belief in free will as truer for one's personal life than determinism.

§ 10

PRACTICAL CONCLUSIONS FROM THESE CONSIDERATIONS

Now what is the practical outcome of all these criticisms of the human mind? Does it follow that thought is futile and discussion vain? By no means. Rather these considerations lead us towards mutual understanding. They clear up the deadlocks that come from the hard and fast use of terms, they establish mutual charity as an intellectual necessity.

The common way of speech and thought which the old system of logic has simply systematized is too glib and too presumptuous of certainty. We must needs use language, but we must use it always with the thought in our minds of its unreal exactness, its actual habitual deflection from fact. All propositions are approximations to an elusive truth, and we employ them as the mathematician studies the circle by supposing it to be a polygon of a very great number of sides.

We must make use of terms and sometimes of provisional terms. But we must guard against such terms and the mental danger of excessive intension they carry with them. The child takes a stick and says it is a sword and does not forget, he takes a shadow under the bed and says it is a bear and he half forgets. The man takes a set of emotions and says it is a God, and he gets excited and propagandist and does forget ; he is involved in disputes and confusions with the old gods of wood and stone, and presently he is making his God a Great White Throne and fitting him up with a mystical family. Yet, because he has made these extravagant extensions of his idea of God, it does not follow that his emotional reaction to a something greater than himself and personal like himself was a deception.

Essentially we have to train our minds to think anew, if we are to think beyond the purposes for which the mind seems to have been evolved. We have to disabuse ourselves from the superstition of the binding nature of definitions and the exactness of logic. We have to cure ourselves of the natural tricks of common thought and argument. You know the way of it, how effective and foolish it is ; the quotation of the exact statement of which every jot and tittle must be maintained, the challenge to be consistent, the deadlock between your terms and mine.

B

More and more as I grow older and more settled in my views am I bored by common argument, bored not because I am ceasing to be interested in the things argued about, but because I see more and more clearly the futility of the methods pursued.

How then are we to think and argue and what truth may we attain? Is not the method of the scientific investigator a valid one, and is there not truth to the world of fact in scientific laws? Decidedly there is. And the continual revision and testing against fact that these laws get is constantly approximating them more and more nearly to a trustworthy statement of fact. Nevertheless they are never true in that dogmatic degree in which they seem true to the unphilosophical student of science. Accepting as I do the validity of nearly all the general propositions of modern science, I have constantly to bear in mind that about them too clings the error of excessive claims to precision.

The man trained solely in science falls easily into a superstitious attitude; he is overdone with classification. He believes in the possibility of exact knowledge everywhere. What is not exact he declares is not knowledge. He believes in specialists and experts in all fields.

I dispute this universal range of possible scientific precision. There is, I allege, a not too clearly recognized order in the sciences which forms the gist of my case against this scientific pretension. There is a gradation in the importance of the individual instance as one passes from mechanics and physics and chemistry through the biological sciences to economics and sociology, a gradation whose correlations and implications have not yet received adequate recognition, and which does profoundly affect the method of study and research in each science.

Let me repeat in slightly altered terms some of

the points raised in the preceding sections. I have doubted and denied that there are identically similar objective experiences ; I consider all objective beings as individual and unique. It is now understood that conceivably only in the subjective world, and in theory and the imagination, do we deal with identically similar units, and with absolutely commensurable quantities. In the real world it is reasonable to suppose we deal at most with *practically* similar units and *practically* commensurable quantities. But there is a strong bias, a sort of labour-saving bias, in the normal human mind, to ignore this, and not only to speak but to think of a thousand bricks or a thousand sheep or a thousand Chinamen as though they were all absolutely true to sample. If it is brought before a thinker for a moment that in any special case this is not so, he slips back to the old attitude as soon as his attention is withdrawn. This type of error has, for instance, caught many of the race of chemists, and *atoms* and *ions* and so forth of the same species are tacitly assumed to be identically similar to one another.

Be it noted that, so far as the practical results of chemistry and physics go, it scarcely matters which assumption we adopt, the number of units is so great, the individual difference so drowned and lost. For purposes of inquiry and discussion the incorrect one is infinitely more convenient.

But this ceases to be true directly we emerge from the region of chemistry and physics. In the biological sciences of the eighteenth century, common sense struggled hard to ignore individuality in shells and plants and animals. There was an attempt to eliminate the more conspicuous departures as abnormalities, as sports, nature's weak moments ; and it was only with the establishment of Darwin's great generalizations that the hard and fast classificatory

system broke down and individuality came to its
own. Yet there had always been a clearly felt
difference between the conclusions of the biological
sciences and those dealing with lifeless substance,
in the relative vagueness, the insubordinate looseness
and inaccuracy of the former. The naturalist
accumulated facts and multiplied names, but he
did not go triumphantly from generalization to
generalization after the fashion of the chemist or
physicist. It is easy to see, therefore, how it came
about that the inorganic sciences were regarded as
the true scientific bedrock. It was scarcely suspected
that the biological sciences might perhaps after all
be *truer* than the experimental, in spite of the difference in practical value in favour of the latter. It was,
and is by the great majority of people to this day,
supposed to be the latter that are invincibly true ;
and the former are regarded as a more complex set
of problems merely, with obliquities and refractions
that presently will be explained away. Comte and
Herbert Spencer certainly seem to me to have taken
that much for granted. Herbert Spencer no doubt
talked of the unknown and unknowable, but not in
this sense as an element of inexactness running
through all things. He thought, it seems to me, of
the unknown as the indefinable Beyond of an immediate world that might be quite clearly and definitely
known.

There is a growing body of people which is beginning to hold the converse view—that counting,
measurement, the whole fabric of mathematics, is
subjective and untrue to the world of fact, and that
the uniqueness of individuals is the objective truth.
They realize that we see this world with " atmosphere." And the number of units taken diminishes,
the amount of variety and inexactness of generalization increases, because individuality tells for more

and more. Could you take men by the thousand billion, you could generalize about them as you do about atoms ; could you take atoms singly, it may be you would find them as individual as your aunts and cousins. That concisely is the minority belief, and my belief.

Now what is called the scientific method in the physical sciences rests upon the ignoring of individualities ; and, like many mathematical conventions, its great practical convenience is no proof whatever of its final truth. Let me admit the enormous value, the wonder of its results in mechanics, in all the physical sciences, in chemistry, even in physiology —but what is its value beyond that ? Is the scientific method of value in biology ? The great advances made by Darwin and his school in biology were not made, it must be remembered, by the scientific method, as it is generally conceived, at all. His was historical research. He conducted a research into pre-documentary history. He collected information along the lines indicated by certain interrogations ; and the bulk of his work was the digesting and critical analysis of that. For documents and monuments he had fossils and anatomical structures and germinating eggs too innocent to lie. But, on the other hand, he had to correspond with breeders and travellers of various sorts ; classes entirely analogous, from the point of view of evidence, to the writers of history and memoirs. I question profoundly whether the word " science," in current usage anyhow, ever means such patient disentanglement as Darwin pursued. It means the attainment of something positive and emphatic in the way of a conclusion, based on amply repeated experiments capable of infinite repetition, " proved," as they say, " up to the hilt."

It would be of course possible to dispute whether

the word "science" should convey this quality of certitude, but to most people it certainly does at the present time. So far as the movements of comets and electric trams go, there is no doubt practically cock-sure science ; and Comte and Herbert Spencer seem to me to have believed that cock-sure could be extended to every conceivable finite thing. The fact that Herbert Spencer called a certain doctrine Individualism reflects nothing on the non-individualizing quality of his primary assumptions and of his mental texture. He believed that individuality (heterogeneity) was and is an evolutionary product from an original homogeneity, begotten by folding and multiplying and dividing and twisting it, and still fundamentally *it*. It seems to me that the popular usage is entirely for the limitation of the word "science" to knowledge of a high degree of precision and the search after knowledge of a high degree of precision.

Now my contention is that we can arrange the fields of human thought and interest about the world of fact in a sort of scale. At one end the number of units is extreme and the methods almost exact, at the other we have the "humanities" in which there is no exactitude. The science of society stands at the extreme end of the scale from the molecular sciences. In these latter there is an infinitude of units ; in sociology, as Comte perceived, there is only one unit. It is true that Herbert Spencer, in order to get classification somehow, did, as Professor Durkheim has pointed out, separate human society into societies, and made believe they competed one with another and died and reproduced just like animals, and that economists following List have for the purposes of fiscal controversy discovered economic types ; but this is a transparent device, and one is surprised to find thoughtful and reputable writers off their guard against such bad analogy. But indeed it is impossible to isolate complete communities of men, or to trace any but rude general resemblances of men, or to trace any but rude general resemblances between group and group. These alleged units have as much individuality as pieces of cloud ; they come, they go, they fuse and separate. And we are forced to conclude that not only is the method of observation, experiment, and verification left far away down the scale, but that the method of classification under types, which has served so useful a purpose in the middle group of subjects, the subjects involving numerous but a finite number of units, has also to be abandoned in social science. We cannot put Humanity into a museum or dry it for examination ; our one single still living specimen is all history, all anthropology, and the fluctuating world of men. There is no satisfactory means of dividing it, and nothing else in the real world with which to compare it. We have only the remotest ideas of its " life-cycle " and a few relics of its origin and dreams of its destiny.

This denial of scientific precision is true of all questions of general human relations and attitude. And in regard to all these matters affecting our personal motives, our self-control and our devotions, it is much truer.

From this it is an easy step to the statement that, so far as the clear-cut confident sort of knowledge goes, the sort of knowledge one gets from a time-table or a textbook of chemistry, or seeks from a witness in a police court, I am, in relation to religious and moral questions, an agnostic. I do not think any general propositions partaking largely of the nature of fact can be known about these things. There is nothing possessing the general validity of fact to be stated or known.

§ 11

BELIEFS

Yet it is of urgent practical necessity that we should have such propositions and beliefs. All those we conjure out of our mental apparatus and the world of fact dissolve and disappear again under scrutiny. It is clear we must resort to some other method for these necessities.

Now I make my beliefs as I want them. I do not attempt to distil them out of fact as physicists distil their laws. I make them thus and not thus exactly as an artist makes a picture so and not so. I believe that is how we all make our beliefs, but that many people do not see this clearly and confuse their beliefs with perceived and proven fact.

I draw my beliefs exactly as an artist draws lines to make a picture, to express my impression of the world and my purpose.

The artist cannot defend his expression as a scientific man defends his, and demonstrate that they are true upon any assumptions whatsoever. Any loud fool may stand in the front of a picture and call it inaccurate, untrustworthy, unbeautiful. That last, the most vital issue of all, is the one least assured. Loud fools always do do that sort of thing. Take quite ignorant people before almost any beautiful work of art and they will laugh at it as absurd. If one sits on a popular evening in that long room at South Kensington which contains Raphael's cartoons, one remarks that perhaps a third of those who stray through and look at all those fine efforts, titter. If one searches in the magazines of a little while ago, one finds in the angry and resentful reception of the Pre-Raphaelites another instance of the absolutely indefensible nature of many of the most beautiful propositions. And as a still more striking and remarkable case, take the onslaught made by Ruskin upon the works of Whistler. You will remember that a libel action ensued and that these pictures were gravely reasoned about by barristers and surveyed by jurymen to assess their merits. . . .

In the end in these human matters it is the truth, however indefensible it may be, however open to blank denials, that lasts; it lasts because it works and serves. People come to it and remain and attract other understanding and inquiring people.

Now when I say I make my beliefs and that I cannot prove them to you and convince you of them, that does not mean that I make them wantonly and regardless of fact, that I throw them off as a child scribbles on a slate. Mr. Ruskin, if I remember rightly, accused Whistler of throwing a pot of paint in the face of the public—that was the essence of his libel. The artistic method in this field of beliefs, as in the field of visual renderings, is one of great freedom and initiative and great poverty of test, but of no wantonness ; the conditions of rightness are none the less imperative because they are mysterious and indefinable. I adopt certain beliefs because I feel the need for them, because I feel an often quite unanalysable rightness in them ; because the alternative of a chaotic life distresses me. My belief in them rests upon the fact that they *work* for me and satisfy my desire for harmony and beauty. They are arbitrary assumptions, if you will, that I see fit to impose upon my universe. But I am not able to go on imposing them upon my universe unless they stand the test of use. With my universe rests the power of veto.

But though my beliefs are really arbitrary in origin, they are not necessarily individual. Just so far as we all have a common likeness, just so

far can we be brought under the same imperatives
to think and believe. Other minds move as mine
does.

And though my beliefs are arbitrary, each day
they stand wear and tear, and each new person they
satisfy, is another day and another voice towards
showing they do correspond to something that is so
far fact and real.

This is Pragmatism as I conceive it : the abandonment of infinite assumptions, the extension of the
experimental spirit to all human interests.

§ 12

THE AIM AND METHOD OF SCIENCE

What I have said so far may seem a little ungra-
cious to Science. It may be well to say a little
more before leaving this metaphysical discussion
altogether, about that new rich store of human knowledge, for the most part the achievement of the last
three hundred years.

My qualification of the scope and exactitude of
science must not be misread into an attack upon
Science. . . .

The scientific process of getting knowledge is really
not different in kind from the method in which
ordinary sensible men have always got knowledge,
and its aim has been very largely the same ; the
difference is that Science is systematic, co-operative
and organized. Science is systematic Classification ;
the ordinary man spends his life working upon classifications unsystematically. But both sorts of judgments are classificatory judgments. The normal
form of ordinary thought is, as I have already in-
sisted in § 5, not syllogism but something after this
form :—

S_1 is P.
S_2 is probably classifiable with S_1.
So S_2 is probably more or less P.
Try it.

Ordinary mental life is constantly making experiments in classification, constantly trying whether S_2 does class in a proper workable way with S_1. Science only differs from this in its patient and systematic hunt for the most working classification, that is to say for the truest classification of things.

There are degrees of value in classification. Let me take a few instances to show what I mean by this.

Take first such a term as " Red Things " or " Old Things." We may speak of such a class as this for the purposes of some special discussion. We may say for instance that red things look black in a blue light. But such a term has scarcely any " intension " at all ; its individuals carry no common property except the property stated in their definition. " Red things " may include a sunset, an angry baby, the planet Mars, a lacquer bowl, a drunkard's nose, and so on and so on. The name " Red-things " is a mere link to hold all this miscellany together for a moment in our minds. Not so do we pack them for good in the pigeon-holes of our brains. There are countless more convenient and useful ways than that.

Next take a term just a little less shallow, a term indicating not one attribute but a use, such as chair. Here the " intension " is a little greater. A small group of characteristics are imposed upon all " chairs " by the conditions of sitting down. Apart from that they are of the most diverse materials, forms, characters and qualities. There is something more real here in the name, in the " term " that holds this collection of things together, but it is still mainly a superficial link behind objects otherwise dissimilar.

The common nouns of our everyday speech record

the classifications of everyday life. They record
the verdict of the people to which we belong upon
what they thought were the working kinds of things.
"Science" is really a persistent criticism and rear-
rangement of these rule-of-thumb workaday classifications. It is a persistent attempt to get to truer
and truer conceptions of the essential kinds of things.
It studied "stuffs," for example; it attacked the
classical idea that the stuffs of the world were made
up of four elements: fire, air, earth, and water. It
broke down the idea that this was a primary classification and it replaced it with a far more accurate
and secure list of elements. Its classification of
fundamental stuffs, albeit it is still remote from any
finality, into carbon, hydrogen, mercury, and so on,
has a far deeper mine of implication, a far keener
statement of difference than the old classification,
and it has yielded such a human mastery over stuffs
and materials as men never dreamt of before the
scientific age. But this newer classification was got
by the organized armies of scientific research exactly
after the fashion in which I get my individual judgments. I see S_2 and something about it suggests to
my mind that it is to be classified with S_1. I know
S_1 is P and so I try if S_2 is P. But while I do this
individually and do not follow it up and forget about
it presently, the organization of research does it
continuingly, records the judgment, confirms it,
reconsiders it and makes sure of it for good. Just
as I impose my arbitrary judgments on the universe,
subject to the veto of the universe (§ 11), so does
Science impose its theories upon the universe subject
to "verification."

Now if the reader will consider the terms that are
used in the sciences of chemistry and mineralogy he
will find that they express a far intenser community
of quality among their individuals, and a far deeper

difference in nature between these individuals and individuals of other species in the same classification, than is the case with the terms of such a use-classification as " Chair," and still more than the terms of such a quality-classification as " Red Thing." The term, the name, is more real. A collection of quartz crystals, for example, have far more in common than a collection of chairs. It is a classification by kind.

Science is perpetually working away from provisional and empirical classifications to classifications of deeper and richer implication. For example, it sets aside such obvious classes as Birds, Beasts and Fishes, and distinguishes mammal from reptile and whale from fish. In the species of biology we get indeed to a maximum of classificatory intensity. The difference between an individual of this species and an individual of that is a difference in every detail and aspect through and through. The common cat and the common rabbit, except for some superficial resemblances, differ in everything ; and every individual in each species agrees with every other individual in that same species upon a thousand matters over and above those specified in the definition, and differs from every individual in every other species. You can tell a cat's claw or hair or one of its small bones, you can tell even a little dried-up drop of its blood from that of a rabbit. Here the term, the specific name, is at its very maximum of reality.

Biological Science does indeed assure us that the distinctness of biological species is exaggerated and emphasized by the disappearance of linking individuals that once bridged the gaps between now separated species. If we could go back in time we should realize that the present sharp distinction of existing biological species melts away in the past. This is a comparatively new idea in human thought. It was natural as well as convenient for man before the scientific era, dealing as he did chiefly with other men and beasts and plants, to form an exaggerated idea of the fixity of classes by kind and to regard the terms, or specific names, that indicated things as having in themselves *reality*.

This was the conception of Plato's Ideals. Besides individual men, Tom Jones, William Smith, and so on, he held that there was an enduring reality, *Man*. Whether this was so or not seems to have been a main subject for discussion in the Middle Ages ; it is a discussion upon which modern biology throws a very strong light, a light so strong indeed as to bleach out many of its difficulties.

§ 13

NOMINALISM AND REALISM

This discussion whether the name of a species expresses something in itself, or whether it is merely a sort of verbal clutch holding together all the individuals of that species and of no other value at all, is one of the perennial questions of philosophy. It crops up in endless variations. It is unavoidable because upon our answer to it depends the meaning of all our religious formulæ and most of our ideas about the relationships of our individual life to the world around it. What are called the " Realists " in the discussions of the Middle Ages, were essentially believers in a rather crude rendering of Platonic Idealism, and it is well to bear this in mind because in modern parlance " Realism " has come to mean something diametrically opposite to its proper significance. The Realists held that the name of a species of things did itself express a reality ; the Nominalists held that the name was merely a link, the string of the bundle of individual things that alone were real.

It will be evident that § 12 has been designed to lead up to the proposition that both these doctrines may be regarded as more or less true according to the nature of the name considered. If the name is the name of an attribute class such as Red-things, it is obviously merely a link ; about such names the Nominalist is right. But as we pass up the scale to biological species we begin to realize that there is a reality transcending the individual and we begin to apprehend the justice of the Realist's arguments so far as classification by kind is concerned. It was chiefly of man that the Greek and mediæval philosophers were thinking ; other things seemed of less significance. They could, they perceived, think of " Man," quite apart from Tom Jones or William Smith ; and so far from thinking of the species man as merely a crowd of individuals, they thought of these individuals as a collection of failures, through this imperfection and that, from the perfect thing Man. Now these discussions of these matters are alien and perplexing to the modern student because he has behind him a century and more of systematized knowledge which makes his attitude to the idea of individuality very different from that of an ancient Greek or a mediæval monk. He is accustomed to think of *Homo sapiens* or *Lepus cuniculus* as the name of a being of a higher order, synthetically speaking, than an individual man or rabbit, a multiple being that maintains itself in its environment, resists adverse forces, and is sustained, modified or exterminated by the outer forces of the universe as time goes on. The reality of the species as a whole is a commonplace in his thought. Having this idea very firmly established in his mind, he is unable to see what these good gentlemen are so earnestly disputing. He is in the position of a far-sighted man who is asked to listen with attention to two shorter-sighted but

revered professors who are discussing very profoundly
whether a distant range of mountains is a bank of
cloud or a dream figment.

§ 14

WHAT IS A BEING?

Human ideas are necessarily anthropocentred, and
man's first idea of unity was the unity of himself.
By the standards of ordinary speech a being is an
entity which can have an independent and complete
relationship to a man; it is capable of a rôle in the
drama of his life. It is unusual to speak of an arm
or a finger or a hat or a ploughed field as a being.
Still less does one think of them as individual beings.
In common speech " an individual " means a human
person. This very natural disposition of the human
mind obsesses much philosophical discussion. On
the other hand, there is a pleasant disposition of vener-
able antiquity to accept individuality in the case
of an animal or a tree or a shapely mountain.
Roughly speaking, the old idea of an individual was
something to which you could pray or at which you
could shake your fist.

Modern scientific work, particularly in the biological sciences, leads to a much keener criticism of
the idea of individuality. Comparative anatomy
leads straight to the discussion, " What is an
individual? " A student drifts easily into the habit
of considering all the larger animals, the metameric
metazoa, as being not so much equivalent to one
individual of the simpler metazoa as to a linear
colony of reduced individuals, and of regarding the
metazoa altogether as equivalent to multiples of
protozoon individuals. He knows that the white
corpuscles in his blood are singularly like individual

amœbas, and that the digestion of every big animal is dependent on the presence of great multitudes of individual bacteria in the intestine. Colonial organizations, the sponges and corals for example, add another aspect to this question. Vegetable individuality is still more disconcerting. What is the individual fungus, is it the toadstool springing from the spreading mycelium or the mycelium, and where is the individuality of a series of grafted trees? Is that three-bladed Irish yew that appeared as a sport years ago and which has been spread by cuttings all round and about the world one individual or many? The mind of the modern biological student is prepared by these things for the idea of individualities of a lower and of a higher order; it can contemplate the possibility of mergers and synthetic formations such as never entered into the heads of the ancient philosophers.

And it is his habit to think of a living species as a single whole, as a synthetic being, unique, conducting a unique struggle against the universe, made up of practically similar but still unique individuals, beings of a less complex grade. In that way also he comes to think of " Man."

§ 15

THE GENERAL AND THE INDIVIDUAL

In our consideration of every person we deal with two aspects. He is William Smith or what not and he is a man. And " William Smith " for him implies everything that is Man in him, but the stress is upon everything that is peculiar and distinctive in him. When we call him a " Man " we thrust these idiosyncrasies into the background and insist upon all those things that he possesses in common with the run of

mankind.   His individuality lies in his difference ;
apart from that he is a sample, a unit of the species.
The life of every William Smith among us has that
double strain ; he is carried along the way of all flesh,
he is a man like other men, and at the same time he
is in every detail just a little different.   By virtue of
that difference and of individual accidents he succeeds
or fails, he survives or is obliterated, he is accepted
into or rejected from the heritage of the race.

At different hours in his life William Smith may be
living with the utmost intensity as William Smith,
or, self-forgetful, as Man.   When he lusts, when he
boasts, when his vanity is bitterly hurt, he is William
Smith *in excelsis*; when he discusses politics or philosophy, or works with delight at a mathematical
problem, he is at his most generalized.   His mind goes
then with the mind of the species; he is Man. . . .
So perhaps in a quite parallel fashion the tissue cells
in our bodies are sometimes full of local and individual
stresses, sometimes altogether absorbed in their
particular services in the common welfare of our
beings.

BOOK THE SECOND

OF BELIEFS

§ I

MY PRIMARY ACT OF FAITH

AND now having stated my conception of the true relationship between our thoughts and words on the one hand and facts on the other, having distinguished between the more accurate and frequently verified propositions of science and the more arbitrary and infrequently verified propositions of belief, and made clear the *spontaneous and artistic quality that inheres in all our moral and religious generalizations*, I may hope to go on to my confession of faith with less misunderstanding than would otherwise be inevitable.

Now my most comprehensive belief about the external and the internal and myself is that they make one universe in which I and every part are ultimately important. That is quite an arbitrary act of my mind. It is quite possible to maintain that everything is a chaotic assembly, that any part might be destroyed without affecting any other part. I do not choose to argue against that. If you choose to say that, I am no more disposed to argue with you than if you choose to wear a mitre in Fleet Street or drink a bottle of ink, or declare the figure of Ally Sloper more dignified and beautiful than the head of Jove. There is no Q.E.D. that you cannot do so. You can. You will not like to go on with it, I think, and it will not answer, but that is a different matter,

I dismiss the idea that life is chaotic because it leaves my life ineffectual, and I cannot contemplate an ineffectual life patiently. I am by my nature impelled to refuse that. I assert that it is not so. I assert therefore that I am important in a scheme, that we all are important in that scheme, that the wheel-smashed frog in the road and the fly drowning in the milk are important and correlated with me. What the scheme as a whole is I do not clearly know; with my limited mind I cannot know. There I become a Mystic. I use the word scheme because it is the best word available, but I strain it in using it. I do not wish to imply a schemer, but only order and co-ordination as distinguished from haphazard. "All this is important, all this is profoundly significant." I say it of the universe as a child that has not learned to read might say it of a parchment agreement. I cannot read the universe, but I can believe that this is so.

And this unfounded and arbitrary declaration of the ultimate rightness and significance of things I call the Act of Faith. It is a voluntary and deliberate determination to believe, a choice made. I do not pretend to be able to prove it. I do not even assert that it is true. It is my working belief.

§ 2

ON USING THE NAME OF GOD

You may say if you will that this scheme I talk about, this something that gives importance and correlation and significance, is what is meant by God. You may embark upon a logical wrangle here with me if you have failed to master what I have hitherto said about the meaning of words. If a Scheme, you will say, then there must be a Schemer.

But, I repeat, I am using scheme and importance and significance here only in a spirit of suggestion because they suggest order and because I can find no better words, and I will not allow myself to be entangled by an insistence upon their implications.

Yet let me confess I am greatly attracted by such fine phrases as the Will of God, the Hand of God, the Great Commander. These do most wonderfully express aspects of this belief I choose to hold. I think if there had been no gods before, I would call this God without hesitation. But there is a great danger in doing this sort of thing unguardedly. The run of people nowadays mean something more and something different when they say " God." They intend a personality exterior to them and limited, and they will instantly conclude I mean the same thing. To permit that misconception is, I feel, the first step on the slippery slope of meretricious complaisance, is to become in some small measure a successor of those who cried, " Great is Diana of the Ephesians!" Occasionally we may best serve the God of Truth by denying him.

Yet at times I admit the sense of personality in the universe is very strong. If I am confessing, I do not see why I should not confess up to the hilt. At times in the silence of the night, and in rare lonely moments, I come upon a sort of communion of myself and something great that is not myself. It is perhaps poverty of mind and language obliges me to say that then this universal scheme takes on the effect of a sympathetic person—and my communion a quality of fearless worship. These moments happen, and they are the supreme fact in my religious life to me, they are the crown of my religious experiences.

None the less, I do not usually speak of God even in regard to these moments, and where I do use that word it must be understood that I use it as a personification of something entirely different in nature from the personality of a human individual.

§ 3

FREE WILL AND PREDESTINATION

And now let me return to a point raised in the First Book in § 9. Is the whole of this scheme of things settled and done? The whole trend of Science is to that belief. On the scientific plane one is a fatalist, the universe a system of inevitable consequences. But as I show in that section referred to, it is quite possible to accept as true in their several planes both predestination and free will.[1] If you ask me, I think I should say I incline to believe in predestination and do quite completely believe in free will. The important working belief is free will.

But does the whole universe of fact, the external world about me, the mysterious internal world from which my motives rise, form one rigid and fated system as determinists teach? Do I believe that, had one a mind ideally clear and powerful, the whole universe would seem orderly and absolutely predestined? I incline to that belief. I do not harshly believe it, but I admit its large plausibility—that is

---

[1] I use free will in the sense of self-determinism and not as it is defined by Professor William James, and predestination as equivalent to the conception of a universe rigid in time and space.

all. I see no value whatever in jumping to a decision. One or two Pragmatists, so far as I can understand them, do not hold this view of predestination at all; but as a provisional assumption it underlies most scientific work.

I glance at this question rather to express a detachment than a view.

For me as a person this theory of predestination has no practical value. At the utmost it is an interesting theory like the theory that there is a fourth dimension. There may be a fourth dimension of space, but one gets along quite well by assuming there are just three. It may be knowable the next time I come to cross roads which I shall take. Possibly that knowledge actually exists somewhere. There are those who will tell you they can get intimations in the matter from packs of cards or the palms of my hands, or see by peering into crystals. Of such beliefs I am entirely free. The fact is I believe that neither I know nor anybody else who is practically concerned knows which I shall take. I hesitate, I choose just as though the thing was unknowable. For me and my conduct there is much wide practical margin of freedom.

I am free and freely and responsibly making the future—so far as I am concerned. You others are equally free. On that theory I find my life will work, and on a theory of mechanical predestination nothing works.

I take the former theory therefore for my everyday purposes and as a matter of working experience so does everybody else. I regard myself as a free responsible person among free responsible persons

§ 4

A PICTURE OF THE WORLD OF MEN

Now I have already given a first picture of the world of fact as it shaped itself upon my mind. Let me now give a second picture of this world in which I find myself, a picture in a rather different key and at a different level, in which I turn to a new set of aspects and bring into the foreground the other minds which are with me in the midst of this great spectacle.

What am I ?

Here is a question to which in all ages men have sought to give a clear unambiguous answer, and to which a clear unambiguous answer is manifestly unfitted. Am I my body ? Yes or no ? It seems to me that I can externalize and think of as " not myself " nearly everything that pertains to my body, hands and feet, and even the most secret and central of those living and hidden parts, the pulsing arteries, the throbbing nerves, the ganglionic centres, that no eye, save for the surgeon's knife, has ever seen or ever will see until they coagulate in decay. So far I am not my body ; and then as clearly, since I suffer through it, see the whole world through it and am always to be called upon where it is, I am it. Am I a mind mysteriously linked to this thing of matter and endeavour ?

So I can present myself. I seem to be a consciousness, vague and insecure, placed between two worlds. One of these worlds seems clearly " not me," the other is more closely identified with me and yet is still imperfectly me. The first I called the exterior world, and it presents itself to me as existing in Time and Space. In a certain way I seem able to interfere with it and control it. The second is the interior world, having no forms in space and only a vague evasive reference to time, from which motives arise and storms of emotion, which acts and reacts constantly and in untraceable ways with my conscious mind. And that consciousness itself hangs and drifts about the region where the inner world and the outer world meet, much as a patch of limelight drifts about the stage, illuminating, affecting, following no manifest law, except that usually it centres about the hero, my Ego.

It seems to me that to put the thing much more precisely than this is to depart from the reality of the matter.

But so departing a little, let me borrow a phrase from Herbart and identify myself more particularly with my mental self. It seems to me that I may speak of myself as a circle of thought and experience poised between these two imperfectly understood worlds of the internal and the external and passing imperceptibly into the former. The external world impresses me as being, as a practical fact, common to me and many other creatures similar to myself; the internal I find similar but not identical with theirs. It is *mine*. It seems to me at times no more than something cut off from that external world and put into a sort of pit or cave, much as all the inner mystery of my body, those living, writhing, warm and thrilling organs, are isolated, hidden from all eyes and interference so long as I remain alive. And I myself, the essential me, am the light and watcher in the mouth of the cave.

So I think of myself, and so I think of all other human beings, as circles of thought and experience, each a little different from the others. Each human being I see as essentially a circle of thought between an internal and an external world.

I figure these circles of thought as more or less

imperfectly focused pictures, all a little askew and vague as to margins and distances. In the internal world arise motives, and they pass outward through the circle of thought and are modified and directed by it into external acts. And through speech, example, and a hundred various acts, one such circle, one human mind, lights and enlarges and plays upon another. That is the image under which the interrelation of minds presents itself to me.

§ 5

THE PROBLEM OF MOTIVES THE REAL PROBLEM OF LIFE

Now each self among us, for all its fluctuations and vagueness of boundary, is, as I have already pointed out, invincibly persuaded of Free Will. That is to say, it has a persuasion of responsible control over the impulses that teem from the internal world and tend to express themselves in act. The problem of that control and its solution is the reality of life. " What am I to do ? " is the perpetual question of our existence. Our metaphysics, our beliefs are all sought as subsidiary to that and have no significance without it.

I confess I find myself a confusion of motives beside which my confusion of perceptions pales into insignificance.

There are many various motives and motives very variously estimated—some are called gross, some sublime, some—such as pride—wicked. I do not readily accept these classifications.

Many people seem to make a selection among their motives without much inquiry, taking those classifications as just ; they seek to lead what they call pure lives or useful lives, and to set aside whole sets

of motives which do not accord with this determination. Some exclude the seeking of pleasure as a
permissible motive, some the love of beauty ; some
insist upon one's " being oneself " and prohibit or
limit responses to exterior opinions. Most of such
selections strike me as wanton and hasty. I decline
to dismiss any of my motives at all in that wholesale
way. Just as I believe I am important in the scheme
of things, so I believe are all my motives. Turning
one's back on any set of them seems to me to savour
of the headlong actions of stupidity. To suppress
a passion or a curiosity for the sake of suppressing a
passion is to my mind just the burial of a talent that
has been entrusted to one's care. One has, I feel,
to take all these things as weapons and instruments,
material in the service of the scheme ; one has to
take them in the end gravely and do right among
them unbiased in favour of any set. To take some
poor appetite and fling it out is to my mind a cheap
and unsatisfactory way of simplifying one's moral
problems. One has to accept these things in oneself,
I feel—even if one knows them to be dangerous things,
even if one is sure they have an evil side.

Let me, however, in order to express my attitude
better, make a rough grouping of the motives I find
in myself and the people about me.

§ 6

A REVIEW OF MOTIVES

I cannot divide them into clearly defined classes
but I may perhaps begin with those that bring one
into the widest sympathy with living things and go
on to those one shares only with more intelligent and
complex creatures.

There come first the desires one shares with those

more limited souls the beasts, just as much as one
does with one's fellow man. These are the bodily
appetites and the crude emotions of fear and resentment. These first clamour for attention and must be
assuaged or controlled before the other sets come
into play.

Now in this matter of physical appetites, I do not
know whether to describe myself as a sensualist or
an ascetic. If an ascetic is one who suppresses to a
minimum all deference to these impulses, then certainly I am not an ascetic ; if a sensualist is one who
gives himself to heedless gratification, then certainly
I am not a sensualist. But I find myself balanced in
an intermediate position by something that I will
speak of as the sense of Beauty. This sense of Beauty
is something in me which demands not simply gratification but the best and keenest of a sense or con-
tinuance of sense impressions, and which refuses
coarse quantitative assuagements. It ranges all
over the senses, and just as I refuse to wholly cut off
any of my motives, so do I refuse to limit its use to
the plane of the eye or the ear.

It seems to me entirely just to speak of beauty in
matters of scent and taste, to talk not only of beautiful skies and beautiful sounds, but of beautiful beer
and beautiful cheese ! The balance as between
asceticism and sensuality comes in, it seems to me,
if we remember that to drink well one must not have
drunken for some time, that to see well one's eye
must be clear, that to make love well one must be
fit and gracious and sweet and disciplined from top
to toe, that the finest sense of all—the joyous sense
of bodily well-being—comes only with exercises and
restraints and fine living. There I think lies the way
of my disposition. I do not want to live in the
sensual sty, but also I do not want to scratch in the
tub of Diogenes.

But I diverge a little in these comments from my present business of classifying motives.

Next I perceive hypertrophied in myself and many sympathetic human beings a passion that many animals certainly possess, the beautiful and fearless cousin of fear, Curiosity, that seeks keenly for knowing and feeling. Apart from appetites and bodily desires and blind impulses, I want most urgently to know and feel, for the sake of knowing and feeling. I want to go round corners and see what is there, to cross mountain ranges, to open boxes and parcels. Young animals at least have that disposition too. For me it is something that mingles with all my desires. Much more to me than the desire to live is the desire to taste life. I am not happy until I have done and felt things. I want to get as near as I can to the thrill of a dog going into a fight or the delight of a bird in the air. And not simply in the heroic field of war and the air do I want to understand. I want to know something of the jolly wholesome satisfaction that a hungry pig must find in its wash.

I do not think that in this I confess to any unusual temperament. I think that the more closely mentally animated people scrutinize their motives the less is the importance they will attach to mere physical and brute urgencies and the more to curiosity.

Next after curiosity come those desires and motives that one shares perhaps with some social beasts, but far more so as a conscious thing with men alone. These desires and motives all centre on a clearly apprehended " self " in relation to " others "; they are the essentially egotistical group. They are self-assertion in all its forms. I have dealt with motives towards gratification and motives towards experience; this set of motives is for the sake of oneself. Since they are the most acutely conscious motives

in unthinking men, there is a tendency on the part
of unthinking people to speak of them as though
vanity, self-seeking, self-interest, were the only
motives. But one has but to reflect on what has gone
before to realize that this is not so. One finds these
" self " motives vary with the mental power and
training of the individual : here they are fragmentary
and discursive, there drawn tight together into a
coherent scheme. Where they are weak they mingle
with the animal motives and curiosity like travellers
in a busy market-place, but where the sense of self
is strong they become rulers and regulators, self-
seeking becomes deliberate and sustained in the case
of the human being, vanity passes into pride.

Here again that something in the mind so difficult
to define, so easy for all who understand to understand, that something which insists upon a best and
keenest, the desire for beauty, comes into the play of
motives. Pride demands a beautiful self and would
discipline all other passions to its service. It also
demands recognition for that beautiful self. Now
pride, I know, is denounced by many as the essential
quality of sin. We are taught that " self-abnegation " is the substance of virtue, and self-forgetfulness
the inseparable quality of right conduct. But
indeed I cannot so dismiss egotism and that pride
which was the first form in which the desire to rule
oneself as a whole came to me. Through pride one
shapes oneself towards a best, though at first it may
be an ill-conceived best. Pride is not always arrogance and aggression. There is that pride that does
not ape but learns humility.

And with the human imagination all these elementary instincts, of the flesh, of curiosity, of self-assertion, become only the basal substance of a huge
elaborate edifice of secondary motive and intention.
We live in a great flood of example and suggestion,

our curiosity and our social quality impel us to a thousand imitations, to dramatic attitudes and subtly obscure ends. Our pride turns this way and that as we respond to new notes in the world about us. We are arenas for a conflict between suggestions flung in from all sources, from the most diverse and essentially incompatible sources. We live long hours and days in a kind of dream, negligent of self-interest, our elementary passions in abeyance, among these derivative things.

§ 7

THE SYNTHETIC MOTIVE

Such it seems to me are the chief masses of the complex of motives in us, the group of sense, the group of pride, curiosity and the imitative and suggested motives, making up the system of impulses which is our will. Such has been the common outfit of motives in every age, and in every age its mêlée has been found insufficient in itself. It is a heterogeneous system, it does not form in any sense a complete or balanced system, its constituents are variable and complete among themselves. They are not so much arranged about one another as superposed and higgledy-piggledy. The senses and curiosity war with pride and one another, the motives suggested to us fall into conflict with this element or that of our intimate and habitual selves. We find all our instincts are snares to excess. Excesses of indulgence lead to excesses of abstinence, and even the sense of beauty may be clouded and betray. So to us, even for the most balanced of us, come disappointments, regrets, gaps ; and for most of us who are ill-balanced, miseries and despairs. Nearly all of us want something to hold us together—something to dominate this swarming confusion and save us from the black misery of wounded and exploded pride, of thwarted desire, of futile conclusions.   We want more oneness, some steadying thing that will afford an escape from fluctuations.

Different people, of differing temperament and tradition, have sought oneness, this steadying and universalizing thing, in various manners. Some have attained it in this manner and some in that. Scarcely a religious system has existed that has not worked effectively and proved true for someone.   To me it seems that the need is synthetic, that some synthetic idea and belief is needed to harmonize one's life, to give a law by which motive may be tried against motive and an effectual peace of mind achieved. I want an active peace and not a quiescence, and I do not want to suppress and expel any motive at all.   But to many people the effort takes the form of attempts to cut off some part of oneself as it were, to repudiate altogether some straining or distressing or disappointing factor in the scheme of motives, and find a tranquillizing refuge in the residuum.   So we have men and women abandoning their share in economic development, crushing the impulses and evading the complications that arise out of sex and flying to devotions and simple duties in nunneries and monasteries ; we have others cutting their lives down to a vegetarian dietary and scientific research, resorting to excesses of self-discipline, giving them-selves up wholly to some " art " and making every-thing else subordinate to that, or, going in another direction, abandoning pride and love in favour of an acquired appetite for drugs or drink.

It seems to me that this desire to get the confused complex of life simplified is essentially what has been called the religious motive, and that the manner in which a man achieves that simplification, if he does achieve it, and imposes an order upon his life, is his religion. I find in the scheme of conversion and salvation, as it is presented by many Christian sects, a very exact statement of the mental processes I am trying to express. In these systems this discontent with the complexity of life upon which religion is based is called the conviction of sin, and it is the first phase in the process of conversion—of finding salvation. It leads through distress and confusion to illumination, to the act of faith and peace.

And after peace comes the beginning of right conduct. If you believe and you are saved, you will want to behave well, you will do your utmost to behave well and to understand what is behaving well and you will feel neither shame nor disappointment when after all you fail. You will say then : " So it is failure I had to achieve." And you will not feel bitterly because you seem unsuccessful beside others or because you are misunderstood or unjustly treated ; you will not bear malice nor cherish anger nor seek revenge ; you will never turn towards suicide as a relief from intolerable things ; indeed, there will be no intolerable things. You will have peace within you.

But if you do not truly believe and are not saved, you will know it because you will still suffer the conflict of motives ; and in regrets, confusions, remorses and discontents, you will suffer the penalties of the unbeliever and the lost. You will know certainly your own salvation.

§ 8

THE BEING OF MANKIND

I will boldly adopt the technicalities of the sects I will speak as a person with experience and declare that I have been through the distresses of despair and the conviction of sin, and that I have found salvation.

I believe in the scheme, in the Project of all things, in the significance of myself and all life, and that my defects and uglinesses and failures, just as much as my powers and successes, are things that are necessary and important and contributory in that scheme, that scheme which passes my understanding—and that no thwarting of my conception, not even the cruelty of nature, now defeats or can defeat my faith, however much it perplexes my mind.

And though I say that scheme passes my understanding, nevertheless I hope you will see no inconsistency when I say that necessarily it has an aspect towards me that I find imperative.

It has an aspect that I can perceive, however dimly and fluctuatingly.

I take it that to perceive this aspect to the utmost of my mental power and to shape my acts according to that perception is my function in the scheme ; that if I hold steadfastly to that conception, I am *saved*. I find in that idea of perceiving the scheme as a whole towards me, and in this attempt to perceive, that something to which all my other emotions and passions may contribute by gathering and contributing experience, and through which the synthesis of my life becomes possible.

Let me try to convey to you what it is I perceive, what aspect this scheme seems to bear on the whole towards me.

The essential fact in man's history to my sense is the slow unfolding of a sense of community with his kind, of the possibilities of co-operations leading to scarce dreamt-of collective powers, of a synthesis of the species, of the development of a common general idea, a common general purpose out of a present confusion. In that awakening of the species, one's own personal being lives and moves—a part of it and contributing to it. *One's individual existence is not so entirely cut off as it seems at first ; one's entirely separate individuality is another, a profounder, among the subtle inherent delusions of the human mind.* Between you and me as we set our minds together, and between us and the rest of mankind, there is *something*, something real, something that rises through us and is neither you nor me, that comprehends us, that is thinking here and using me and you to play against each other in that thinking just as my finger and thumb play against each other as I hold this pen with which I write.

Let me point out that this is no sentiment~~ or mystical statement. It is hard fact as any hard fact we know. We, you and I, are not only parts in a thought process, but parts of one flow of blood and life. Let me put that in a way that may be new to some readers. Let me remind you of what is sometimes told as a jest, the fact that the number of one's ancestors increases as we look back in time. Disregarding the chances of intermarriage, each one of us had two parents, four grandparents, eight great-grandparents, and so on backward, until very soon, in less than fifty generations, we should find that, but for the qualification introduced, we should have all the earth's inhabitants of that time as our progenitors. For a hundred generations it must hold absolutely true that every one of that time who has issue living now is ancestral to all of us. That brings the thing quite within the historical period. There is not a western European palæolithic or neolithic relic of the present human race that is not a family relic for every soul alive. The blood in our veins has handled it.

And there is something more. We are all going

to mingle our blood again. We cannot keep ourselves apart ; the worst enemies will some day come to the Peace of Verona. All the Montagues and Capulets are doomed to intermarry. A time will come in less than fifty generations when all the population of the world will have my blood, and I and my worst enemy will not be able to say which child is his or mine.

But you may retort—perhaps you may die child-less. Then all the sooner the whole species will get the little legacy of my personal achievement, what-ever it may be.

You see that from this point of view—which is for me the vividly true and dominating point of view—our individualities, our nations and states and races, are but bubbles and clusters of foam upon the great stream of the blood of the species, incidental experiments in the growing knowledge and conscious-ness of the race.

I think this real solidarity of humanity is a fact that is only being slowly apprehended, that it is an idea that we who have come to realize it have to assist in thinking into the collective mind. I believe the species is still as a whole unawakened, still sunken in the delusion of the permanent separateness of the individual and of races and nations, that so it turns upon itself and frets against itself and fails to see the stupendous possibilities of deliberate self-develop-ment that lie open to it now.

I see myself in life as part of a great physical being that strains and I believe grows towards beauty, and of a great mental being that strains and I believe grows towards knowledge and power. In this per-suasion that I am a gatherer of experience, a mere tentacle that arranges thought beside thought for this being of the species, this being that grows beauti-ful and powerful, in this persuasion I find the ruling idea of which I stand in need, the ruling idea that reconciles and adjudicates among my warring motives. In it I find both concentration of myself and escape from myself; in a word, I find Salvation.

§ 9

INDIVIDUALITY AN INTERLUDE

I would like in a parenthetical section to expand and render rather more concrete this idea of the species as one divaricating flow of blood, by an appeal to its arithmetical aspect. I do not know if it has ever occurred to the reader to compute the number of his living ancestors at some definite date, at, let us say, the year 1 of the Christian era. Every one has two parents and four grandparents, and most people have eight great-grandparents, and if we ignore the possibility of intermarriage we shall go on to a fresh power of two with every generation, thus :—

3	8
4	16
5	32
7	128
10	1,024
20	1,048,576
30	1,073,741,824
40	1,099,511,627,776

I do not know whether the average age of the parent at the birth of a child under modern conditions can be determined from existing figures. There is, I should think, a strong presumption that it has been a rising age. There may have been a time in the past when most women were mothers in their early teens and bore most or all of their children before thirty, and when men had done the greater part of their procreation before thirty-five; this is still the case in many tropical climates, and I do not think I favour my case unduly by assuming that the average parent must be about, or even less than, five-and-twenty. This gives four generations to a century. At that rate and *disregarding intermarriage of relations* the ancestors living a thousand years ago needed to account for a living person would be many times the estimated population of the world. But it is obvious that if a person sprang from a marriage of first cousins, the eight ancestors of the third generation are cut down to six ; if of cousins at the next stage, to fourteen in the fourth. And every time that a common pair of ancestors appears in any generation, the number of ancestors in that generation must be reduced by two from our original figures, or if it is only one common ancestor, by one, and as we go back that reduction will have to be doubled, quadrupled, and so on. I dare say that by the time anyone gets to the 8,192 names of his Elizabethan ancestors he will find quite a large number repeated over and over again in the list and that he is cut down to perhaps two or three thousand separate persons. But this does not effectually invalidate my assumption that if we go back only to the closing years of the Roman Republic, we go back to an age in which nearly every person living within the confines of what was then the Roman Empire who left living offspring must have been ancestral to every person living within that area to-day. No doubt they were so in very variable measure. There must be for every one some few individuals in that period who have, so to speak, intermarried with themselves again and again and again down the genealogical series, and others who are represented by just one touch of their blood. The blood of the Jews, for example, has turned in upon itself again and again ; but for all we know one Italian proselyte in the first year of the Christian era may have made by this time every Jew alive a descendant of some unrecorded bastard of Julius Cæsar. The exclusive breeding of the Jews is in fact the most effectual guarantee that whatever does get into the charmed circle through either proselytism, the violence of enemies, or feminine unchastity, must ultimately pervade it universally.

It may be argued that as a matter of fact humanity has until recently been segregated in pools ; that in the great civilization of China, for example, humanity has pursued its own interlacing system of inheritances without admixture from other streams of blood. But such considerations only defer the conclusion ; they do not stave it off indefinitely. It needs only that one philoprogenitive Chinaman should have wandered into those regions that are now Russia, about the time of Pericles, to link east and west in that matter ; one Tartar chieftain in the Steppes may have given a daughter to a Roman soldier and sent his grandsons east and west to interlace the branches of every family tree in the world. If any race stands apart it is such an isolated group as that of the now extinct Tasmanian primitives or the Australian black. But even here, in the remote dawn of navigation, may have come some shipwrecked Malays, or some half-breed woman kidnapped by wandering Phœnicians have carried this link of blood back to the western world. The more one lets one's imagination play upon the incalculable drift and soak of population, the more one realizes the true value of that spreading relation with the past.

But now let us turn in the other direction, the direction of the future, because there it is that this series of considerations becomes most edifying. It is the commonest trick to think of a man's descendants as though they were his own. We are told that one of the dearest human motives is the desire to found a family, but think how much of a family one founds at the best. One's son is after all only half one's blood, one's grandson only a quarter, and so one goes on until it may be that in ten brief generations one's heir and namesake has but $\frac{1}{1024}$th of one's inherited self. Those other thousand odd unpredictable people thrust in and mingle with one's pride. The trend of all things nowadays—the ever-increasing ease of communication, the great and increasing drift of population, the establishment of a common standard of civilization—is to render such admixture far more probable and facile in the future than in the past.

It is a pleasant fancy to imagine some ambitious hoarder of wealth, some egotistical founder of name and family, returning to find his descendants—*his* descendants—after the lapse of a few brief generations. His heir and namesake may have not a thousandth part of his heredity, while under some other name, lost to all the tradition and glory of him, enfeebled and degenerate through much intermarriage, may be a multitude of people who have as much as a fiftieth or even more of his quality. They may even be in servitude and dependence to the really alien person who is head of the family. Our founder will go through the spreading record of offspring and find it mixed with that of people he most hated and despised. The antagonists he wronged and overcame will have crept into his line and recaptured all they lost ; have played the cuckoo in his blood and acquisitions, and turned out his diluted strain to perish.

And while I am being thus biological let me point out another queer aspect in which our egotism is overridden by physical facts. Men and women are apt to think of their children as being their very own, blood of their blood and bone of their bone. But indeed one of the most striking facts in this matter is the frequent want of resemblance between parents and children. It is one of the commonest things in the world for a child to resemble an aunt or an uncle, or to revive a trait of some grandparent that has seemed entirely lost in the intervening generation. The Mendelians have given much attention to facts of this nature ; and though their general method of exposition seems to me quite unjustifiably exact and precise, it cannot be denied that it is often vividly illuminating. It is so in this connection. They distinguish between "dominant" and "recessive" qualities, and they establish cases in which parents with all the dominant characteristics produce offspring of recessive type. Recessive qualities are constantly being masked by dominant ones and emerging again in the next generation. It is not the individual that reproduces himself, it is the species that reproduces through the individual and often in spite of his characteristics.

The race flows through us, the race is the drama and we are the incidents. This is not any sort of poetical statement ; it is a statement of fact. In so far as we are individuals, in so far as we seek to follow merely individual ends, we are accidental, disconnected, without significance, the sport of chance. In so far as we realize ourselves as experiments of the species for the species, just in so far do we escape from the accidental and the chaotics. We are episodes in an experience greater than ourselves.

Now none of this, if you read me aright, makes for the suppression of one's individual difference, but it does make for its correlation. We have to get everything we can out of ourselves for this very reason that we do not stand alone ; we signify as parts of a universal and immortal development. Our separate selves are our charges, the talents of which much has to be made. It is because we are episodical in the great synthesis of life that we have to make the utmost of our individual lives and traits and possibilities.

§ 10

THE MYSTIC ELEMENT

What stupendous constructive mental and physical possibilities are there to which I feel I am contributing, you may ask, when I feel that I contribute to this greater Being; and at once I confess I become vague and mystical. I do not wish to pass glibly over this point. I call your attention to the fact that here I am mystical and arbitrary. I am what I am, an individual in this present phase. I can see nothing of these possibilities except that they will be in the nature of those indefinable and overpowering gleams of promise in our world that we call Beauty. Elsewhere (in my " Food of the Gods ") I have tried to render my sense of our human possibility by monstrous images; I have written of those who will " stand on this earth as on a footstool and reach out their hands among the stars." But that is rhetoric at best, a straining image of unimaginable things. Things move to Power and Beauty; I say that much and I have said all that I can say.

But what is Beauty, you ask, and what will Power do? And here I reach my utmost point in the direction of what you are free to call the rhapsodical and the incomprehensible. I will not even attempt to define Beauty. I will not because I cannot. To me it is a final, quite indefinable thing. Either you understand it or you do not. Every true artist and many who are not artists know—they know there is something that shows suddenly—it may be in music, it may be in painting, it may be in the sunlight on a glacier or shadow cast by a furnace or the scent of a flower, it may be in the person or act of some fellow creature, but it is right, it is commanding, it is, to use theological language, the revelation of God. To this mystery of Power and Beauty, out of the earth that mothered us, we move.

I do not attempt to define Beauty nor even to distinguish it from Power. I do not think indeed that one can effectually distinguish these aspects of life. I do not know how far Beauty may not be simply fullness and clearness of sensation, a momentary unveiling of things hitherto seen but dully and darkly. As I have already said, there may be beauty in the feeling of beer in the throat, in the taste of cheese in the mouth ; there may be beauty in the scent of earth, in the warmth of a body, in the sensation of waking from sleep. I use the word Beauty therefore in its widest possible sense, ranging far beyond the special beauties that art discovers and develops. Perhaps as we pass from death to life all things become beautiful. The utmost I can do in conveying what I mean by Beauty is to tell of things that I have perceived to be beautiful as beautifully as I can tell of them. It may be, as I suggest elsewhere, that Beauty is a thing synthetic and not simple ; it is a common effect produced by a great medley of causes, a larger aspect of harmony.

But the question of what Beauty is does not very greatly concern me since I have known it when I met it and since almost every day in life I seem to apprehend it more and to find it more sufficient and satisfying. Objectively it may be altogether complex and various and synthetic, subjectively it is altogether simple. All analysis, all definition, must in the end rest upon and arrive at unanalysable and indefinable things. Beauty is light—I fall back upon that image—it is all things that light can be, beacon, elucidation, pleasure, comfort and consolation, promise, warning, the vision of reality.

§ 11

THE SYNTHESIS

It seems to me that the whole living creation may be regarded as walking in its sleep, as walking in the sleep of instinct and individualized illusion, and that now out of it all rises the Spirit of Man, beginning to perceive his larger self, his collective synthetic purpose to increase Power and realize Beauty. . . .

I write this down. It is the form of my belief, and that unanalysable something called Beauty is the light that falls upon that great figure.

It is only by such images, it is only by the use of what are practically parables, that I can in any way express these things in my mind. These two things, I say, are the two aspects of my belief; one is the form and the other the light. The former places me as it were in a scheme, the latter illuminates and inspires me. I am a member in that greater Being, and my function is, I take it, to develop my capacity for beauty and convey the perception of it to my fellows to gather and store experience and increase the racial consciousness. I hazard no whys nor wherefores. That is how I see things; that is how the universe, in response to my demand for a synthesizing aspect, presents itself to me. I see it as the scene of the great adventure of the human spirit, that God of Man, of which I am servant and part.

§ 12

OF PERSONAL IMMORTALITY

These are my beliefs. They begin with arbitrary assumptions; they end in mystery.

So do all beliefs that are not grossly utilitarian

and material, promising houris and deathless appetite
or endless hunting or a cosmic mortgage. The Peace
of God passeth understanding, the Kingdom of
Heaven within us and without can be presented only
by parables. But the unapproachable distance and
vagueness of these things makes them none the less
necessary, just as a cloud upon a mountain, or sunlight remotely seen upon the sea, is as real as, and to
many people far more necessary than, pork chops.
The driven swine may root and take no heed, but
man the dreamer drives. And because these things
are vague and impalpable and wilfully attained, it
is none the less important that they should be rendered
with all the truth of one's being. To be atmospheric-
ally vague is one thing ; to be haphazard, wanton and
untruthful, quite another.

But here I may give a specific answer to a question
that many find profoundly important, though indeed it
is already implicitly answered in what has gone before.

I do not believe I have any personal immortality.
I am part of an immortality perhaps ; but that is
different. I personally am not the continuing thing.
I am experimental, incidental. I feel I have to do
something, a number of things no one else could do,
and then I am finished, and finished altogether.
Then my substance returns to the common lot. I
am a temporary enclosure for a temporary purpose ;
that served, and my skull and teeth, my idiosyncrasy
and desire, will disperse, I believe, like the timbers
of a booth after a fair.

Let me shift my ground a little and ask you to
consider what is involved in the opposite belief.

My idea of the unknown scheme is of something
so wide and deep that I cannot conceive it encum-
bered by my egotism perpetually. I shall serve my
purpose and pass under the wheel and end. That
distresses me not at all. Immortality would distress

and perplex me.   If I may put this in a mixture of theological and social language, I cannot respect, I cannot believe in a God who is always going about with me.

But this is after all what I feel is true and what I choose to believe.   It is not a matter of fact.   So far as that goes there is no evidence that I am immortal and none that I am not.

I may be altogether wrong in my beliefs ; I may be misled by the appearance of things.   I believe in the great and growing Being of the Species from which I rise, to which I return, and which, it may be, will ultimately even transcend the limitation of the Species and grow into the Conscious Being, the undying conscious Being of all things.   Believing that, I cannot also believe that my peculiar little thread will not undergo synthesis and vanish as a separate thing.

And what after all is my distinctive something, a few capacities, a few incapacities, an uncertain memory, a hesitating presence ?   It matters no doubt in its place and time, as all things matter in their place and time, but where in it all is the eternally indispensable ?   The great things of my life, love, saith, and intimation of beauty, the things most favouring of immortality, are the things most general, the things most shared and least distinctively me.

§ 13

A CRITICISM OF CHRISTIANITY

And here perhaps, before I go on to the question of Conduct, is the place to define a relationship to that system of faith and religious observance out of which I and most of my readers have come.   How do these beliefs on which I base my rule of conduct stand to Christianity ?

They do not stand in any attitude of antagonism. A religious system so many-faced and so enduring as Christianity must necessarily be saturated with truth even if it be not wholly true. To assume, as the Atheist and Deist seem to do, that Christianity is a sort of disease that came upon civilization, an unprofitable and wasting disease, is to deny that conception of a progressive scheme and rightness which we have taken as our basis of belief. As I have already confessed, the Scheme of Salvation, the idea of a process of sorrow and atonement, presents itself to me as adequately true. So far I do not think my new faith breaks with my old. But it follows as a natural consequence of my metaphysical preliminaries that I should find the Christian theology, Aristotelian, over defined and excessively personified. The painted figure of that bearded ancient upon the Sistine Chapel, or William Blake's wild-haired, wild-eyed Trinity, convey no nearer sense of God to me than some mother-of-pearl-eyed painted and carven monster from the worship of the South Sea Islanders. And the Miltonic fable of the offended creator and the sacrificial son ! it cannot span the circle of my ideas ; it is a little thing, and none the less little because it is intimate, flesh of my flesh and spirit of my spirit, like the drawings of my youngest boy. I put it aside as I would put aside the gay figure of a costumed officiating priest. The passage of time has made his canonicals too strange, too unlike my world of common thought and costume. These things helped, but now they hinder and disturb. I cannot bring myself back to them.

But the psychological experience and the theology of Christianity are only a groundwork for its essential feature, which is the conception of a relationship of the individual believer to a mystical being at once human and divine, the Risen Christ. This being pre-

sents itself to the modern consciousness as a familiar
and beautiful figure, associated with a series of say-
ings and incidents that coalesce with a very distinct
and rounded-off and complete effect of personality.
After we have cleared off all the definitions of theology, He remains, mystically suffering for humanity,
mystically asserting that love in pain and sacrifice in
service are the necessary substance of Salvation.
Whether he actually existed as a finite individual
person in the opening of the Christian era seems to
me a question entirely beside the mark. The evidence at this distance is of imperceptible force for
or against. The Christ we know is quite evidently
something different from any finite person, a figure,
a conception, a synthesis of emotions, experiences
and inspirations, sustained by and sustaining millions
of human souls.

Now it seems to be the common teaching of almost
all Christians that Salvation, that is to say the con-
solidation and amplification of one's motives through
the conception of a general scheme or purpose, is to
be attained through the personality of Christ. Christ
is made cardinal to the act of Faith. The act of
Faith, they assert, is *belief in Him*.

We are dealing here, be it remembered, with beliefs deliberately undertaken and not with questions
of fact. The only matters of fact material here are
facts of experience. If in your experience Salvation
is attainable through Christ, then certainly Christianity is true for you. And if a Christian asserts
that my belief is a false light and that presently I
shall " come to Christ," I cannot disprove his asser-
tion. I can but disbelieve it. I hesitate even to
make the obvious retort.

I hope I shall offend no susceptibilities when I
assert that this great and very definite personality
in the hearts and imaginations of mankind does not

and never has attracted me. It is a fact I record about myself without aggression or regret. I do not find myself able to associate Him with the emotion of Salvation.

I admit the splendid imaginative appeal in the idea of a divine-human friend and mediator. If it were possible to have access by prayer, by meditation, by urgent outcries of the soul, to such a being whose feet were in the darknesses, who stooped down from the light, who was at once great and little, limitless in power and virtue and one's very brother; if it were possible by sheer will in believing to make and make one's way to such a helper, who would refuse such help? But I do not find such a being in Christ. To me the Christian Christ seems not so much a humanized God as an incomprehensibly sinless being neither God nor man. His sinlessness wears his incarnation like a fancy dress, all his white self unchanged. He had no petty weaknesses.

Now the essential trouble of my life is its petty weaknesses. If I am to have that love, that sense of understanding fellowship, which is, I conceive, the peculiar magic and merit of this idea of a personal Saviour, then I need someone quite other than this image of virtue, this terrible and incomprehensible Galilean with his crown of thorns, his blood-stained hands and feet. I cannot love him any more than I can love a man upon the rack. Even in the face of torments I do not think I should feel a need for him. I had rather then a hundred times have Botticelli's armed angel in his Tobit at Florence. (I hope I do not seem to want to shock in writing these things, but indeed my only aim is to lay my feelings bare.) I know what love for an idealized person can be. It happens that in my younger days I found a character in the history of literature who had a singular and extraordinary charm for me, of whom the thought was tender and comforting, who indeed helped me through shames and humiliations as though he held my hand. This person was Oliver Goldsmith. His blunders and troubles, his vices and vanities, seized and still hold my imagination. The slights of Boswell, the contempt of Gibbon and all his company save Johnson, the exquisite fineness of spirit in his *Vicar of Wakefield*, and that green suit of his and the doctor's cane and the love despised, these things together made him a congenial saint and hero for me, so that I thought of him as others pray. When I think of that youthful feeling for Goldsmith, I know what I need in a personal Saviour, as a troglodyte who has seen a candle can imagine the sun. But the Christian Christ in none of his three characteristic phases, neither as the magic babe (from whom I am cut off by the wanton and indecent purity of the Virgin Birth), nor as the white-robed, spotless miracle-worker, nor as the fierce unreal torment of the cross, comes close to my soul. I do not understand the Agony in the Garden ; to me it is like a scene from a play in an unknown tongue. The last cry of despair is the one human touch, discordant with all the rest of the story. One cry of despair does not suffice. The Christian's Christ is too fine for me, not incarnate enough, not flesh enough, not earth enough. He was never foolish and hot-eared and inarticulate, never vain, he never forgot things, nor tangled his miracles. I could love him I think more easily if the dead had not risen and if he had lain in peace in his sepulchre instead of coming back more enhaloed and whiter than ever, as a postscript to his own tragedy.

When I think of the Resurrection I am always reminded of the " happy endings " that editors and actor managers are accustomed to impose upon essentially tragic novels and plays. . . .

You see how I stand in this matter, puzzled and confused by the Christian presentation of Christ. I know there are many will answer that what confuses me is the overlaying of the personality of Jesus by stories and superstitions and conflicting symbols; they will in effect ask me to disentangle the Christ I need from the accumulated material, choosing and rejecting. Perhaps one may do that. They do, I know, so present Him as a man inspired, and strenuously, inadequately and erringly presenting a dream of human brotherhood and the immediate Kingdom of Heaven on earth and so blundering to his failure and death. But that will be a recovered and restored person they would give me, and not the Christ the Christians worship and declare they love, in whom they find their Salvation.

When I write "declare they love" I throw doubt intentionally upon the universal love of Christians for their Saviour. I have watched men and nations in this matter. I am struck by the fact that so many Christians fall back upon more humanized figures, upon the tender figure of Mary, upon patron saints and such more erring creatures, for the effect of mediation and sympathy they need.

You see it comes to this : that I think Christianity has been true and is for countless people practically true, but that it is not true now for me, and that for most people it is true only with qualifications. Every believing Christian is, I am sure, my spiritual brother, but if systematically I called myself a Christian I feel that to most men I should imply too much and so tell a lie.

§ 14

OF OTHER RELIGIONS

In the same manner, in varying degree, I hold all religions to be in a measure true. Least comprehensible to me are the Indian formulæ, because they seem to stand not on common experience but on those intellectual assumptions my metaphysical analysis destroys. Transmigration of souls without a continuing memory is to my mind utter foolishness, the imagining of a race of children. The aggression, discipline and submission of Mohammedanism makes, I think, an intellectually limited but fine and honourable religion—for men. Its spirit if not its formulæ is abundantly present in our modern world. Mr. Rudyard Kipling, for example, manifestly preaches a Mohammedan God, a modernized Allah with a taste for engineering. I have no doubt that in devotion to a virile, almost national Deity and to the service of His Empire of stern Law and Order, efficiently upheld, men have found and will find Salvation.

All these religions are true for me as Canterbury Cathedral is a true thing and as a Swiss chalet is a true thing. There they are, and they have served a purpose, they have worked. Men and women have lived in and by them. Men and women still do. Only they are not true for me to live in them. I have, I believe, to live in a new edifice of my own discovery. They do not work for me.

These schemes are true, and also these schemes are false! in the sense that new things, new phrasings, have to replace them.

BOOK THE THIRD

OF GENERAL CONDUCT

§ 1

CONDUCT FOLLOWS FROM BELIEF

THE broad direction of conduct follows necessarily from belief. The believer does not require rewards and punishments to direct him to the right. Motive and idea are not so separable. To believe truly is to want to do right. To get salvation is to be unified by a comprehending idea of a purpose and by a ruling motive.

The believer wants to do right, he naturally and necessarily seeks to do right. If he fails to do right, if he finds he has done wrong instead of right, he is not greatly distressed or terrified, he naturally and cheerfully does his best to correct his error. He can be damned only by the fading and loss of his belief. And naturally he recurs to and refreshes his belief.

I write in phrases that the evangelical Christianity of my childhood made familiar to me, because they are the most expressive phrases I have ever met for the psychological facts with which I am dealing.

But faith, though it banishes fear and despair and brings with it a real pervading desire to know and do the Good, does not in itself determine what is the Good or supply any simple guide to the choice between alternatives. If it did, there would be nothing more to be said, this book upon conduct would be unnecessary.

§ 2

WHAT IS GOOD?

It seems to me one of the heedless errors of those who deal in philosophy, to suppose all things that have simple names or unified effects are in their nature simple and may be discovered and isolated as a sort of essence by analysis. It is natural to suppose—and I think it is also quite wrong to suppose—that such things as Good and Beauty can be abstracted from good and beautiful things and considered alone. But pure Good and pure Beauty are to me empty terms. It seems to me that these are in their nature synthetic things, that they arise out of the coming together of contributory things and conditions, and vanish at their dispersal; they are synthetic just as more obviously Harmony is synthetic. It is consequently not possible to give a definition of Good, just as it is not possible to give a definition of that other something which is so closely akin to it, Beauty. Nor is it to be maintained that what is good for one is good for another. But what is good of one's general relations and what is right in action must be determined by the nature of one's beliefs about the purpose in things. I have set down my broad impression of that purpose in respect to me, as the awakening and development of the consciousness and will of our species, and I have confessed my belief that in subordinating myself and all my motives to that idea lies my Salvation. It follows from that that the good life is the life that most richly gathers and winnows and prepares experience and renders it available for the race, that contributes most effectively to the collective growth.

This is in general terms my idea of Good. So soon as one passes from general terms to the question of individual good, one encounters individuality; for every one in the differing quality and measure of their personality and powers and possibilities, good and right must be different. We are all engaged, each contributing from his or her own standpoint, in the collective synthesis; whatever one can best do, one must do that; in whatever manner one can best help the synthesis, one must exert oneself; the setting apart of oneself, secrecy, the service of secret and personal ends, is the waste of life and the essential quality of Sin.

That is the general expression for right living as I conceive it. In such terms it may be expressed, but also it may be expressed in far more living words. For this collective " synthesis " is the adventure of humanity, the " purpose in things " is no more and no less than the enterprise of God the captain of mankind.

§ 3

SOCIALISM

In the study of God's will in us, it is very convenient to make a rough division of our subject into general and particular. There are first the interests and problems that affect us all collectively, in which we have a common concern and from which no one may legitimately seek exemption; of these interests and problems we may fairly say every man should do so and so, or so and so, or the law should be so and so, or so and so; and, secondly, there are those other problems in which individual difference and the interplay of one or two individualities is predominant. This is of course no hard and fast classification, but it gives a method of approach. We can begin with the generalized person in ourselves and end with individuality.

In the world of ideas about me, I have found going on a great social and political movement that correlates itself with my conception of God's service as the aspect towards us of the general human scheme. This movement is Socialism. Socialism is to me no clear-cut system of theories and dogmas; it is one of those solid and extensive and synthetic ideas that are better indicated by a number of different formulæ than by one, just as one only realizes a statue by walking round it and seeing it from a number of points of view. I do not think it is to be completely expressed by any one system of formulæ or by any one man. Its common quality from nearly every point of view is the subordination of the will of the self-seeking individual to the idea of a racial well-being embodied in an organized state under God, organized for every end that can be best obtained collectively. Upon that I seize; that is the value of Socialism for me.

Socialism for me is a common step we are all taking in the realization of God's purpose of human organization and unity. It is the organization of the general effort in regard to a great mass of common and fundamental interests that have hitherto been dispersedly served.

I see humanity scattered over the world, dispersed, conflicting, unawakened. . . . I see human life as avoidable waste and curable confusion. I see peasants living in wretched huts knee-deep in manure, mere parasites on their own pigs and cows; I see shy hunters wandering in primeval forests; I see the grimy millions who slave for industrial production;

I see some who are extravagant and yet contemptible
creatures of luxury, and some leading lives of shame
and indignity ; tens of thousands of wealthy people
wasting lives in vulgar and unsatisfying trivialities,
hundreds of thousands meanly chaffering themselves,
rich or poor, in the wasteful byways of trade ; I see
gamblers, fools, brutes, toilers, martyrs. Their disorder of effort, the spectacle of futility is an offence
against God, and fills the believer with a passionate
desire to end waste, to create order, to develop understanding. . . . All these people reflect and are part
of the waste and discontent of life. The co-ordination of the species to a common general end, and the
quest for a personal salvation, are the two aspects,
the outer and the inner, the social and the individual
aspect of essentially the same desire. . . .

And yet dispersed as all these people are, they are
far more closely drawn together to common ends and
a common effort than the filthy savages who ate food
rotten and uncooked in the age of unpolished stone.
They live in the mere opening phase of a synthesis of
effort the end of which surpasses our imagination.
Such intercourse and community as they have is only
a dawn. We look towards the day, the day of the
earthly Kingdom of God, the organized civilized
world state. The first clear intimation of that conscious synthesis of human thought to which I look,
the first edge of the dayspring, has arisen—as Socialism, as I conceive of Socialism. Socialism is to me
no more and no less than the realization of a common
end, universal loyalty in mankind, the awakening of
a collective consciousness of duty in humanity, the
awakening of a collective will and a collective mind
out of which finer individualities may arise for ever
in a perpetual series of fresh endeavours and fresh
achievements for the race.

§ 4

A CRITICISM OF CERTAIN FORMS OF SOCIALISM

It seems to me one of the heedless errors arising in this way out of the conception of a synthesis of the will and thought of the species will necessarily differ from conceptions of Socialism arrived at in other and different ways. It is based on a self-discontent and self-abnegation and not on self-satisfaction, and it will be essentially a scheme of persistent thought and construction ; it will support this or that method of law-making, or this or that method of economic exploitation, or this or that matter of social grouping, only incidentally and in relation to that.

Such a conception of Socialism is very remote in spirit, however it may agree in method, from that philanthropic administrative socialism one finds among the British ruling administrative class. That seems to me to be based on a pity which is largely unjustifiable and a pride that is altogether unintelligent. The pity is for the obvious wants and distresses of poverty, the pride appears in the arrogant and aggressive conception of raising one's fellows. I have no strong feeling for the horrors and discomforts of poverty as such, sensibilities can be hardened to endure the life led by the *Romans* in Dartmoor jail a hundred years ago,[1] or softened to detect the crumpled rose-leaf ; what disgusts me is the stupidity and warring purposes of which poverty is the outcome. When it comes to this idea of raising human beings, I must confess the only person I feel concerned about raising is H. G. Wells, and that even in his case my energies might be better employed. After all, presently he must die and the world will

[1] See *The Story of Dartmoor Prison*, by Basil Thomson (Heinemann—1907).

have done with him. His output for the species is more important than his individual elevation.

Moreover, all this talk of raising implies a classification I doubt. I find it hard to fix any standards that will determine who is above me and who below. Most people are different from me, I perceive, but which among them is better, which worse ? I have a certain power of communicating with other minds, but what experiences I communicate seem often far thinner and poorer stuff than those which others less expressive than I half fail to communicate and half display to me. My " inferiors," judged by the common social standards, seem indeed intellectually more limited than I and with a narrower outlook ; they are often dirtier and more driven, more under the stress of hunger and animal appetites ; but, on the other hand, have they not more vigorous sensations than I, and, through sheer coarsening and hardening of fibre, the power to do more toilsome things and sustain intenser sensations than I could endure ? When I sit upon the bench, a respectable magistrate, and commit some battered reprobate for trial for this lurid offence or that, or send him or her to prison for drunkenness or such-like indecorum, the doubt drifts into my mind which of us after all is indeed getting nearest to the keen edge of life. Are I and my respectable colleagues much more than successful evasions of *that* ? Perhaps these people in the dock know more of the essential strains and stresses of nature, are more intimate with pain. At any rate I do not think I am justified in saying certainly that they do not know. . . .

No, I do not want to raise people using my own position as a standard, I do not want to be one of a gang of consciously superior people, I do not want arrogantly to change the quality of other lives. I do not want to interfere with other lives, except inci-

dentally—incidentally in this way that I do want to
get an understanding with them. I do want to share
and feel with them in our commerce with the collective mind. I suppose I do not stretch language very
much when I say I want to get rid of stresses and
obstacles between our minds and personalities and to
establish a relation that is understanding and sympathy and that will bring us at last to the harmonious
service of God.

I want to make more generally possible a relationship of communication and interchange, that for want
of a less battered and ambiguous word I must needs
call love.

And if I disavow the Socialism of condescension, so
also do I disavow the Socialism of revolt. There is a
form of Socialism based upon the economic generalizations of Marx, an economic fatalistic Socialism that
I hold to be rather wrong in its vision of facts, rather
more distinctly wrong in its theory, and altogether
wrong and hopeless in its spirit. It preaches, as inevitable, a concentration of property in the hands of
a limited number of property owners and the expro-
priation of the great proletarian mass of mankind, a
concentration which is after all no more than a tendency conditional on changing and changeable conventions about property, and it finds its hope of a
better future in the outcome of a class conflict between the expropriated Many and the expropriating
Few. Both sides are to be equally swayed by self-
interest, but the toilers are to be gregarious and mutually loyal in their self-interest—Heaven knows why,
except that otherwise the Marxist dream will not
work. The experience of contemporary events seems
to show at least an equal power of combination for
material ends among owners and employers as among
workers.

Now this class-war idea is one diametrically opposed to that religious-spirited Socialism which supplies the form of my general activities. This class-war idea would exacerbate the antagonism of the interests of the many individuals against the few individuals, and I would oppose the service of the Whole to the self-seeking of the Individual. The spirit and constructive intention of the many to-day are no better than those of the few, poor and rich alike are over-individualized, self-seeking and non-creative; to organize the confused jostling competitions, over-reachings, envies and hatreds of to-day into two great class-hatreds and antagonisms will advance the reign of love at most only a very little, only so far as it will simplify and make plain certain issues. It may very possibly not advance the reign of love at all, but rather shatter the order we have. Socialism, as I conceive it, seeks to change economic arrangements only by the way, as an aspect and outcome of a great change, a change in the spirit and method of human intercourse, a change from an individual claim to a claim to serve the Spirit of Mankind fully and completely.

I know that here I go beyond the limits many Socialists in the past, and some who are still contemporary, have set for themselves. Much Socialism to-day seems to think of itself as fighting a battle against poverty and its concomitants alone. Now poverty is only a symptom of a profounder evil and is never to be cured by itself. It is one aspect of divided and dispersed purposes. If Socialism is only a conflict with poverty, Socialism is nothing. But I hold that Socialism is and must be a battle against human stupidity and egotism and disorder, a battle fought all through the forests and jungles of the soul of man. As we get intellectual and moral light and the realization of brotherhood, so social and economic organization will develop. But the Socialist may attack poverty for ever, disregarding the intellectual and moral factors that necessitate it, and he will remain until the end a purely economic doctrinaire crying in the wilderness in vain.

And if I antagonize myself in this way to the philanthropic Socialism of kindly prosperous people on the one hand and to the fierce class-hatred Socialism on the other, still more am I opposed to that furtive Socialism of the specialist which one meets most typically in the Fabian Society. It arises very naturally out of what I may perhaps call specialist fatigue and impatience. It is very easy for writers like myself to deal in the broad generalities of Socialism and urge their adoption as general principles ; it is altogether another affair with a man who sets himself to work out the riddle of the complications of actuality in order to modify them in the direction of Socialism. He finds himself in a jungle of difficulties that strain his intellectual power to the utmost. He emerges at last with conclusions, and they are rarely the obvious conclusions, as to what needs to be done. Even the people of his own side he finds do not see as he sees ; they are, he perceives, crude and ignorant.

Now I hold that his duty is to explain his discoveries and intentions until they see as he sees. But the specialist temperament is often not a generalizing and expository temperament. Specialists are apt to measure minds by their speciality and underrate the average intelligence. The specialist is appalled by the real task before him, and he sets himself by tricks and misrepresentations, by benevolent scoundrelism in fact, to effect changes he desires. Too often he fails even in that. Where he might have found fellowship he arouses suspicion. And even if a thing is done in this way, its essential merit is lost. For it is better, I hold, for a man to die of his disease than to be cured unwittingly. That is to cheat him of life and to cheat life of the contribution his consciousness might have given it.

The Socialism of my beliefs rests on a profounder faith and a broader proposition. It looks over and beyond the warring purposes of to-day as a general may look over and beyond a crowd of sullen, excited and confused recruits, to the day when they will be disciplined, exercised, trained, willing and convergent on a common end. It holds persistently to the idea of men increasingly working in agreement, doing things that are sane to do, on a basis of mutual helpfulness, temperance and toleration. It sees the great masses of humanity rising out of base and immediate anxieties, out of dwarfing pressures and cramped surroundings, to understanding and participation and fine effort. It sees the resources of the earth husbanded and harvested, economized and used with scientific skill for the maximum of result. It sees towns and cities finely built, a race of beings finely bred and taught and trained, open ways and peace and freedom from end to end of the earth. It sees beauty increasing in humanity, about humanity and through humanity. Through this great body of mankind goes evermore an increasing understanding, an intensifying brotherhood. As Christians have dreamt of the New Jerusalem so does Socialism, growing evermore temperate, patient, forgiving and resolute, set its face to the World City of Mankind.

§ 5

HATE AND LOVE

Before I go on to point out the broad principles of action that flow from this wide conception of Socialism, I may perhaps give a section to elucidating that opposition of hate and love I made when I dealt with the class war. I have already used the word love several times ; it is an ambiguous word and it may be well to spend a few words in making clear the sense in which it is used here. I use it here in a broad sense to convey all that complex of motives, impulses, sentiments, that incline us to find our happiness and satisfactions in the happiness and sympathy of others and to merge ourselves emotionally in a design greater than ourselves. Essentially it is a synthetic force in human affairs, the merger tendency, a linking force, an expression in personal will and feeling of the common element and interest. It insists upon resemblances and shares and sympathies. And hate, I take it, is the emotional aspect of antagonism, it is the expression in personal will and feeling of the individual's separation from others. It is the competing and destructive tendency. So long as we are individuals and members of a species, we must needs both hate and love. But because I believe, as I have already confessed, that the oneness of the species is a greater fact than individuality, and that we individuals are temporary separations from a collective purpose, and since hate eliminates itself by eliminating its objects, whilst love multiplies itself by multiplying its objects, so love must be a thing more comprehensive and enduring than hate.

Moreover, hate must be in its nature a good thing. We individuals exist as such, I believe, for the purpose in things, and our separations and antagonisms serve that purpose. We play against each other like hammer and anvil. But the synthesis of a collective will in humanity, which is I believe our human and terrestrial share in that purpose, is an idea that carries with it a conception of a secular alteration in the scope and method of both love and hate. Both widen and change with man's widening and developing apprehension of the purpose he serves. The savage man loves in gusts a fellow creature or so about him, and fears and hates all other people. Every expansion of his scope and ideas widens either circle. The common man of our civilized world loves not only many of his friends and associates systematically and enduringly, but dimly he loves also his city and his country, his creed and his race ; he loves it may be less intensely but over a far wider field and much more steadily. But he hates also more widely if less passionately and vehemently than a savage, and since love makes rather harmony and peace and hate rather conflicts and events, one may easily be led to suppose that hate is the ruling motive in human affairs. Men band themselves together in leagues and loyalties, in cults and organizations and nationalities, and it is often hard to say whether the bond is one of love for the association or hatred of those to whom the association is antagonized. The two things pass insensibly into one another. London people have recently seen an instance of the transition, in the Brown Dog statue riots (1908). A number of people drawn together by their common pity for animal suffering, by love indeed of the most disinterested sort, had so forgotten their initial spirit as to erect a monument with an inscription at once recklessly untruthful, spiteful in spirit and particularly vexatious to one great medical school of London. They have provoked riots and placarded London with taunts and irritating misrepresentation of the spirit of medical research, and they have infected a whole fresh generation of London students with a bitter partisan contempt for the humanitarian effort that has so lamentably misconducted itself. Both sides vow they will never give in, and the antivivisectionists are busy manufacturing small china copies of the Brown Dog figure, inscription and all, for purposes of domestic irritation. Here hate, the evil ugly

D

brother of effort, has manifestly slain love the initi-
ator and taken the affair in hand. That is a little
model of human conflicts. So soon as we become
militant and play against one another, comes this
danger of strain and this possible reversal of motive.
The fight begins. Into a pit of heat and hate fall
right and wrong together.

Now it seems to me that a religious faith such as I
have set forth in the Second Book, and a clear sense
of our community of blood with all mankind, must
necessarily affect both our loving and our hatred. It
will certainly not abolish hate, but it will subordinate
it altogether to love. We are individuals, so the
Purpose presents itself to me, in order that we may
hate the things that have to go, ugliness, baseness,
insufficiency, unreality, that we may love and experiment and strive for the things that collectively we
seek—power and beauty. Before our conversion we
did this darkly and with our hate spreading to persons and parties from the things for which they stood.
But the believer will hate lovingly and without fear.
We are of one blood and substance with our antagonists, even with those that we desire keenly may die
and leave no issue in flesh or persuasion. They all
touch us and are part of one necessary experience.
They are all necessary to the synthesis, even if they
are necessary only as the potato-peel in the dust-bin
is necessary to my dinner.

So it is I disavow and deplore the whole spirit of
class-war Socialism with its doctrine of hate, its
envious assault upon the leisure and freedom of the
wealthy. Without leisure and freedom and the
experience of life they gave, the ideas of Socialism
could never have been born. The true mission of
Socialism is against darkness, vanity and cowardice,
that darkness which hides from the property owner
the intense beauty, the potentialities of interest, the

splendid possibilities of life, that vanity and cowardice that make him clutch his precious holdings and fear and hate the shadow of change. It has to teach the collective organization of society; and to that the class-consciousness and intense class-prejudices of the worker need to bow quite as much as those of the property owner. But when I say that Socialism's mission is to teach, I do not mean that its mission is a merely verbal and mental one ; it must use all instruments and teach by example as well as precept. Socialism by becoming charitable and merciful will not cease to be militant. Socialism must, lovingly but resolutely, use law, use force, to dispossess the owners of socially disadvantageous wealth, as one coerces a lunatic brother or takes a wrongfully acquired toy from a spoiled and obstinate child. It must intervene between all who would keep their children from instruction in the business of citizenship and the lessons of fraternity. It must build and guard what it builds with laws and with that sword which is behind all laws. Non-resistance is for the non-constructive man, for the hermit in the cave and the naked saint in the dust ; the builder and maker with the first stroke of his foundation spade uses force and opens war against the anti-builder.

§ 6

THE PRELIMINARY SOCIAL DUTY

The belief I have that contributing to the development of the collective being of man is the individual's general meaning and duty, and the formulæ of the Socialism which embodies this belief so far as our common activities go, give a general framework and direction how a man or woman should live. (I do throughout all this book mean man or woman equally when I write of " man," unless it is manifestly inapplicable.)

And first in this present time he must see to it that he does live, that is to say he must get food, clothing, covering, and adequate leisure for the finer aspects of living. Socialism plans an organized civilization in which these things will be a collective solicitude, and the gaining of a subsistence an easy preliminary to the fine drama of existence, but in the world as we have it we are forced to engage much of our energy in scrambling for these preliminary necessities. Our problems of conduct lie in the world as it is and not in the world as we want it to be. First then a man must get a living, a fair, civilized living for himself. It is a fundamental duty. It must be a fair living, not pinched nor mean nor strained. A man can do nothing higher, he can be of no service to any cause, until he himself is fed and clothed and equipped and free. He must earn this living or equip himself to earn it in some way not socially disadvantageous, he must contrive as far as possible that the work he does shall be constructive and contributory to the general well-being.

And these primary necessities of food, clothing and freedom being secured, one comes to the general disposition of one's surplus energy. With regard to that I think that a very simple proposition follows from the broad beliefs I have chosen to adopt. The general duty of a man, his existence being secured, is to educate, and chiefly to educate and develop himself. It is his duty to live, to make all he can out of himself and life, to get full of experience, to make himself fine and perceiving and expressive, to render his experience and perceptions honestly and helpfully to others. And in particular he has to educate himself and others with himself in Socialism. He has to make and keep this idea of synthetic human effort and of

conscious constructive effort clear first to himself and
then clear in the general mind.   For it is an idea that
comes and goes.   We are all of us continually lapsing
from it towards individual isolation again.   He needs,
we all need, constant refreshment in this belief if it
is to remain a predominant living fact in our lives.

And that duty of education, of building up the collective idea and organization of humanity, falls into
various divisions depending in their importance upon
individual quality.   For all there is one personal work
that none may evade, and that is thinking hard, criti-
cizing strenuously and understanding as clearly as
one can religion, socialism and the general principle
of one's acts.   The intellectual factor is of primary
importance in my religion.   I can see no more reason
why salvation should come to the intellectually incapable than to the morally incapable.   For simple
souls thinking in simple processes, salvation perhaps
comes easily, but there is none for the intellectual
coward, for the mental sloven and sluggard, for the
stupid and obdurate mind.   The Believer will think
hard and continue to grow and learn, to read and
seek discussion as his needs determine.

Correlated with one's own intellectual activity,
part of it and growing out of it for almost every one,
is intellectual work with and upon others.   By teaching we learn.   Not to communicate one's thoughts to
others, to keep one's thoughts to oneself as people
say, is either cowardice or pride.   It is a form of sin.
A good man is an open man.   It is a duty to talk,
teach, explain, write, lecture, read, and listen.   Every
truly religious man, every good Socialist, is a propagandist.   Those who cannot write or discuss can talk,
those who cannot argue can induce people to listen
to others and read.   We have a belief and an idea
that we want to spread, each to the utmost of his
means and measure, throughout all the world.   We

have a thought that we want to make humanity's thought. And it is a duty too that one should, within the compass of one's ability, make teaching, writing and lecturing possible where it has not existed before. This can be done in a hundred ways, by founding and enlarging schools and universities and chairs, for example; by making print and reading and all the material of thought cheap and abundant, by organizing discussion and societies for inquiry.

And talk and thought and study are but the more generalized aspects of duty. The Believer may find his own special aptitude lies rather among concrete things, in experimenting and promoting experiments in collective action. Things teach as well as words, and some of us are most expressive by concrete methods. The Believer will work himself and help others to his utmost in all those developments of material civilization, in organized sanitation for example, all those developments that force collective acts upon communities and collective realizations into the minds of men. And the whole field of scientific research is a field of duty calling to everyone who can enter it, to add to the permanent store of knowledge and new resources for the race.

The Mind of that Civilized State we seek to make by giving ourselves into its making, is evidently the central work before us. But while the writer, the publisher and printer, the bookseller and librarian and teacher and preacher, the investigator and experimenter, the reader and everyone who thinks, will be contributing themselves to this great organized mind and intention in the world, many sorts of specialized men will be more immediately concerned with parallel and more concrete aspects of the human synthesis. The medical worker and the medical investigator, for example, will be building up the body of a new generation, the body of the civilized state, and he will be doing all he can, not simply as an individual, but as a citizen, to *organize* his services of cure and prevention, of hygiene and selection. A great and growing multitude of men will be working out the apparatus of the civilized state ; the organizers of transit and housing, the engineers in their incessantly increasing variety, the miners and geologists estimating the world's resources in metals and minerals, the mechanical inventors perpetually economizing force. The scientific agriculturist, again, will be studying the food supply of the world as a whole, and how it may be increased and distributed and economized. And to the student of law comes the task of rephrasing his intricate and often quite beautiful science in relation to modern conceptions. All these and a hundred other aspects are integral to the wide project of Constructive Socialism as it shapes itself in my faith.

§ 7

WRONG WAYS OF LIVING

When we lay down the proposition that it is one's duty to get one's living in some way not socially disadvantageous, and as far as possible by work that is contributory to the general well-being and development, when we state that one's surplus energies, after one's living is gained, must be devoted to experience, self-development and constructive work, it is clear we condemn by implication many modes of life that are followed to-day.

For example, it is manifest we condemn living in idleness or on non-productive sport, on the income derived from private property, and all sorts of ways of earning a living that cannot be shown to conduce to the constructive process. We condemn trading that is merely speculative, and in fact all trading and manufacture that is not a positive social service ; we condemn living by gambling or by playing games for either stakes or pay.   Much more do we condemn dishonest or fraudulent trading and every act of advertisement that is not punctiliously truthful.   We must condemn too the taking of any income from the community that is neither earned nor conceded in the collective interest.   But to this last point, and to certain issues arising out of it, I will return in the section next following this one.

And it follows evidently from our general propositions that every form of prostitution is a double sin, against one's individuality and against the species which we serve by the development of that individuality's preferences and idiosyncrasies.

And by prostitution I mean not simply the act of a woman who sells for money, and against her thoughts and preferences, her smiles and endearments and the secret beauty and pleasure of her body, but the act of anyone who, to gain a living, suppresses himself, does things in a manner alien to himself and subserves aims and purposes with which he disagrees. The journalist who writes against his personal convictions, the solicitor who knowingly assists the schemes of rogues, the barrister who pits himself against what he perceives is justice and the right, the artist who does unbeautiful things or less beautiful things than he might, simply to please base employers, the craftsman who makes instruments for foolish uses or bad uses, the dealer who sells and pushes an article because it fits the customer's folly : all these are prostitutes of mind and soul if not of body, with no right to lift an eyebrow at the painted disasters of the streets.

§ 8

These broad principles about one's way of living
are very simple ; our minds move freely among them.
But the real interest is with the individual case, and
the individual case is almost always complicated by
the fact that the existing social and economic system
is based upon conditions that the growing collective
intelligence condemns as unjust and undesirable, and
that the constructive spirit in men now seeks to
supersede. We have to live in a provisional State
while we dream of and work for a better one.

The ideal life for the ordinary man in a civilized,
that is to say a Socialist, State would be in public
employment or in private enterprise aiming at public
recognition. But in our present world only a small
minority can have that direct and honourable relation of public service in the work they do ; most of
the important business of the community is done
upon the older and more tortuous private ownership
system, and the great mass of men in socially useful
employment find themselves working only indirectly
for the community and directly for the profit of a
private owner, or they themselves are private owners.
Every man who has any money put by in the bank,
or any money invested, is a private owner, and in so
far as he draws interest or profit from this investment
he is a social parasite. It is in practice almost impossible to divest oneself of that parasitic quality, however straightforward the general principle may be.

It is practically impossible for two equally valid
sets of reasons. The first is that, under existing conditions, saving and investment constitute the only
way to rest and security in old age, to leisure, study
and intellectual independence, to the safe upbringing

of a family and the happiness of one's weaker depen-
dents. These are things that should not be left for
the individual to provide ; in the civilized State, the
State itself will insure every citizen against these
anxieties that now make the study of the City Article
almost a duty. To abandon saving and investment
to-day, and to do so is of course to abandon all insur-
ance, is to become a driven and uncertain worker, to
risk one's personal freedom and culture and the upbringing and efficiency of one's children. It is to
lower the standard of one's personal civilization, to
think with less deliberation and less detachment, to
fall away from that work of accumulating fine habits
and beautiful and pleasant ways of living contributory to the coming State. And in the second place
there is not only no return for such a sacrifice in anything won for Socialism, but for fine-thinking and
living people to give up property is merely to let it
pass into the hands of more egoistic possessors. Since
at present things must be privately owned, it is
better that they should be owned by people consciously working for social development and willing
to use them to that end.

We have to live in the present system and under
the conditions of the present system, while we work
with all our power to change that system for a better
one.

The case of Cadburys the cocoa and chocolate
makers, and the practical slavery under the Portuguese of the East African negroes who grow the raw
material for Messrs. Cadbury, is an illuminating one
in this connection. The Cadburys, like the Rown-
trees, are well known as an energetic and public-
spirited family, their social and industrial experiments at Bournville and their general social and
political activities are broad and constructive in the
best sense. But they find themselves in the peculiar

dilemma that they must either abandon an important and profitable portion of their great manufacture or continue to buy produce grown under cruel and even horrible conditions. Their retirement from the branch of the cocoa and chocolate trade concerned would, under these circumstances, mean no diminution of the manufacture or of the horrors of this particular slavery; it would mean merely that less humanitarian manufacturers would step in to take up the abandoned trade. The self-righteous individualist would have no doubts about the question; he would keep his hands clean anyhow, retrench his social work, abandon the types of cocoa involved, and pass by on the other side. But indeed I do not believe we came into the mire of life simply to hold our hands up out of it. Messrs. Cadbury follow a better line; they keep their business going, and exert themselves in every way to let light into the secrets of Portuguese East Africa and to organize a better control of these labour cruelties. That I think is altogether the right course in this difficulty.

We cannot keep our hands clean in this world as it is. There is no excuse indeed for a life of fraud or any other positive fruitless wrong-doing or for a purely parasitic non-productive life, yet all but the fortunate few who are properly paid and recognized state servants must in financial and business matters do their best amidst and through institutions tainted with injustice and flawed with unrealities. All Socialists everywhere are like expeditionary soldiers far ahead of the main advance. The organized state that should own and administer their possessions for the general good has not arrived to take them over; and in the meanwhile they must act like its anticipatory agents according to their lights and make things ready for its coming.

The Believer then who is not in the public service,

whose life lies among the operations of private enterprise, must work always on the supposition that the
property he administers, the business in which he
works, the profession he follows, is destined to be
taken over and organized collectively for the com-
monweal and must be made ready for the taking
over ; that the private outlook he secures by investment, the provision he makes for his friends and
children, are temporary, wasteful, though at present
unavoidable devices to be presently merged in and
superseded by the broad and scientific previsions of
the co-operative commonwealth.

§ 9

THE CASE OF THE WIFE AND MOTHER

These principles give a rule also for the problem
that faces the great majority of thinking wives and
mothers to-day. The most urgent and necessary
social work falls upon them ; they bear, and largely
educate and order the homes of, the next generation,
and they have no direct recognition from the community for either of these supreme functions. They are
supposed to perform them not for God or the world,
but to please and satisfy a particular man. Our
laws, our social conventions, our economic methods,
so hem a woman about that, however fitted for
and desirous of maternity she may be, she can only
effectually do that duty in a dependent relation to
her husband. Nearly always he is the paymaster,
and if his payments are grudging or irregular, she
has little remedy short of a breach and the rupture
of the home. Her duty is conceived of as first to him
and only secondarily to her children and the State.
Many wives become, under these circumstances, mere
prostitutes to their husbands, often evading the

bearing of children with their consent, and even at
their request, and " loving for a living." That is a
natural outcome of the proprietary theory of the
family out of which our civilization emerges. But
our modern ideas trend more and more to regard a
woman's primary duty to be her duty to the children
and to the world to which she gives them. She is
to be a citizen side by side with her husband ; no
longer is he to intervene between her and the community. As a matter of contemporary fact he can
do so and does so habitually, and most women
have to square their ideas of life to that possibility.

Before any woman who is clear-headed enough to
perceive that this great business of motherhood is
one of supreme public importance, there are a number of alternatives at the present time. She may,
like Grant Allen's heroine in *The Woman Who
Did*, declare an exaggerated and impossible independence, refuse the fetters of marriage and bear
children to a lover. This, in the present state of
public opinion in almost every existing social atmosphere, would be a purely anarchistic course. It
would mean a fatherless home, and since the woman
will have to play the double part of income-earner
and mother, an impoverished and struggling home.
It would mean also an unsocial because ostracized
home. In most cases, and even assuming it to be
right in idea, it would still be on all fours with that
immediate abandonment of private property we have
already discussed, a sort of suicide that helps the
world nothing.

Or she may " strike," refuse marriage and pursue
a solitary and childless career, engaging her surplus
energies in constructive work. But that also is
suicide ; it is to miss the keenest experiences, the
finest realities life has to offer.

Or she may meet a man whom she can trust to keep a treaty with her and supplement the common interpretations and legal insufficiencies of the marriage bond, who will respect her always as a free and independent person, will abstain absolutely from authoritative methods, and will either share and trust his income and property with her in a frank communism, or give her a sufficient and private income for her personal use. It is only fair under existing economic conditions that at marriage a husband should insure his life in his wife's interest, and I do not think it would be impossible to bring our legal marriage contract into accordance with modern ideas in that matter. Certainly it should be legally imperative that at the birth of each child a new policy upon its father's life, as the income-getter, should begin. The latter provision at least should be a normal condition of marriage and one that a wife should have power to enforce when payments fall away. With such safeguards and under such conditions marriage ceases to be a haphazard dependence for a woman, and she may live, teaching and rearing and free, almost as though the co-operative commonwealth had come.

But in many cases, since great numbers of women marry so young and so ignorantly that their thinking about realities begins only after marriage, a woman will find herself already married to a man before she realizes the significance of these things. She may be already the mother of children. Her husband's ideas may not be her ideas. He may dominate, he may prohibit, he may intervene, he may default. He may, if he sees fit, burthen the family income with the charges of his illegitimate offspring. He may by his will deprive wife and children of any share of the family property.

We live in the world as it is and not in the world

as it should be. That sentence becomes the refrain of this discussion.

The normal modern married woman has to make the best of a bad position, to do her best under the old conditions, to live as though she was under the new conditions, to make good citizens, to give her spare energies as far as she can to bringing about a better state of affairs. Like the private property owner and the official in a privately owned business, her best method of conduct is to consider herself an unrecognized public official, irregularly commanded and improperly paid. There is no good in flagrant rebellion. She has to study her particular circumstances and make what good she can out of them, keeping her face towards the coming time. I cannot better the image I have already used for the thinking and believing modern-minded people of to-day as an advance guard cut off from proper supplies, ill furnished so that makeshift prevails, and rather demoralized. We have to be wise as well as loyal; discretion itself is loyalty to the coming State.

§ 10

OF ABSTINENCES AND DISCIPLINES

I have already confessed that my nature is one that dislikes abstinences and is wearied by and wary of excess.

I do not feel that it is right to suppress altogether any part of one's being. In itself abstinence seems to me a refusal to experience, and that, upon the lines of thought I follow, is to say that abstinence for its own sake is evil. But for an end all abstinences are permissible, and if the kinetic type of believer finds both his individual and his associated efficiency enhanced by a systematic discipline, if he

is convinced that he must specialize because of the
discursiveness of his motives, because there is something he wants to do or be so good that the rest of
them may very well be suppressed for its sake, then
he must suppress.   But the virtue is in what he gets
done and not in what he does not do.   Reasonable
fear is a sound reason for abstinence, as when a man
has a passion like a lightly sleeping maniac that the
slightest indulgence will arouse.   Then he must needs
adopt heroic abstinence, and even more so must he
take to preventive restraint if he sees any motive
becoming unruly and urgent and troublesome.   Fear
is a sound reason for abstinence, and so is love.   Many
who have sensitive imaginations nowadays very
properly abstain from meat because of butchery.
And it is often needful, out of love and brotherhood,
to abstain from things harmless to oneself because
they are inconveniently alluring to others linked to
us.   The moderate drinker who sits at table sipping
his wine in the sight of one he knows to be a poten-
tial dipsomaniac is at the best an unloving fool.

But mere abstinence and the doing of barren toilsome unrewarding things for the sake of the toil, is
a perversion of one's impulses.   There is neither
honour nor virtue nor good in that.

I do not believe in negative virtues.   I think the
ideas of them arise out of the system of metaphysical
errors I have roughly analysed in my First Book, out
of the inherent tendency of the mind to make the
relative absolute and to convert quantitative into
qualitative differences.   Our minds fall very readily
under the spell of such unmitigated words as Purity
and Chastity.   Only death beyond decay, absolute
non-existence, can be Pure and Chaste.   Life is impurity, fact is impure.   Everything has traces of alien
matter ; our very health is dependent upon parasitic
bacteria ; the purest blood in the world has a tainted

ancestor, and not a saint but has evil thoughts. It was blindness to that which set men stoning the woman taken in adultery. They forgot what they were made of. This stupidity, this unreasonable idealism of the common mind, fills life to-day with cruelties and exclusions, with partial suicides and secret shames. But we are born impure, we die impure ; it is a fable that spotless white lilies sprang from any saint's decay, and the chastity of monk or nun is but introverted impurity. We have to take life valiantly on these conditions and make such honour and beauty and sympathy out of our confusions, gather such constructive experience, as we may.

There is a mass of real superstition upon these points, a belief in a magic purity, in magic personalities who can say—

> My strength is as the strength of ten
> Because my heart is pure,

and wonderful clairvoyant innocents like the young man in Mr. Kipling's *Finest Story in the World.*

There is a lurking disposition to believe, even among those who lead the normal type of life, that the abstinent and chastely celibate are exceptionally healthy, energetic, immune. The wildest claims are made. But indeed it is true for all who can see the facts of life simply and plainly that man is an omnivorous, versatile, various creature and can draw his strength from a hundred varieties of nourishment. He has physiological idiosyncrasies too that are indifferent to biological classifications and moral generalities. It is not true that his absorbent vessels begin their task as children begin the guessing game, by asking, " Is it animal, vegetable, or mineral ? " He responds to stimulation and recuperates after the exhaustion of his response, and his being is singularly careless whether the stimulation comes as a drug or stimulant, or as anger or music or noble appeals.

Most people speak of drugs in the spirit of that admirable firm of soap-boilers which assures its customers that the soap they make "contains no chemicals." Drugs are supposed to be a mystic diabolical class of substance, remote from and contrasting in their nature with all other things. So people banish a tonic from the house and stuff their children with manufactured cereals and chocolate-creams. The drunken helot of this system of absurdities is the Christian Scientist who denies healing only to those who have studied pathology, and declares that anything whatever put into a bottle and labelled with directions for its use by a doctor is thereby damnable and damned. But indeed all drugs and all the things of life have their uses and dangers, and there is no wholesale truth to excuse us a particular wisdom and watchfulness in these matters. Unless we except smoking as an unclean and needless artificiality, all these matters of eating and drinking and habit are matters of more or less. It seems to me foolish to make anything that is stimulating and pleasurable into a habit, for that is slowly and surely to lose a stimulus and pleasure and create a need that it may become painful to check or control. The moral rule of my standards is irregularity. If I were a father confessor I should begin my catalogue of sins by asking : "Are you a man of regular life ?" And I would charge my penitent to go away forthwith and commit some practicable saving irregularity ; to fast or get drunk or climb a mountain or sup on pork and beans or give up smoking or spend a month with publicans and sinners. Right conduct for the common unspecialized man lies delicately adjusted between defect and excess as a watch is adjusted and adjustable between fast and slow. We none of us altogether and always keep the balance or are altogether safe from losing it. We swing, balancing and adjusting, along our path. Life is that, and abstinence is for the most part a mere evasion of life.

§ 11

ON FORGETTING, AND THE NEED OF PRAYER, READING, DISCUSSION AND WORSHIP

One aspect of life I had very much in mind when I planned those Samurai disciplines of mine. It was forgetting.

We forget. Even after we have found Salvation, we have to keep hold of Salvation; believing, we must continue to believe. We cannot always be at a high level of noble emotion. We have clambered on the ship of Faith and found our place and work aboard, and even while we are busied upon it, behold we are back and drowning in the sea of chaotic things.

Every religious body, every religious teacher, has appreciated this difficulty, and the need there is of reminders and renewals. Faith needs restatement and revival as the body needs food. And since the Believer is to seek much experience and be a judge of less or more in many things, it is particularly necessary that he should keep hold upon a living Faith.

How may he best do this?

I think we may state it as a general duty that he must do whatever he can to keep his faith constantly alive. But beyond that, what a man must do depends almost entirely upon his own intellectual character. Many people of a regular type of mind can refresh themselves by some recurrent duty, by repeating a daily prayer, by daily reading or re-reading some devotional book. With others constant repetition leads to a mental and spiritual deadening, until beautiful phrases become unmeaning, eloquent statements inane and ridiculous—matter for parody. All who can, I think, should pray and should read and re-read what they have found spiritually helpful, and if they know of others of kindred dispositions and can organize these exercises, they should do so. Collective worship again is a necessity for many Believers. For many, the public religious services of this or that form of Christianity supply an atmosphere rich in the essential quality of religion and abounding in phrases about the religious life, mellow from the use of centuries and almost immediately applicable. It seems to me that if one can do so, one should participate in such public worship and habituate oneself to read back into it that collective purpose and conscience it once embodied.

Very much is to be said for the ceremony of Holy Communion or the Mass, for those whom accident or intellectual scruples do not debar. I do not think young modern liberal thinkers quite appreciate the finer aspects of this, the one universal service of the Christian Church. Some of them are set forth very finely by a man who has been something of a martyr for conscience' sake, and is for me a hero as well as a friend, in a world not rich in heroes,[1] the Rev. Stewart Headlam, in his book, *The Meaning of the Mass*.

With others again, Faith can be most animated by writing, by confession, by discussion, by talk with friends or antagonists.

One or other or all of these things the Believer must do, for the mind is a living and moving process, and the thing that lies inert in it is presently covered up by new interests and lost. If you make a sort of King Log of your faith, presently something else will

[1] Obviously written in 1908.

be sitting upon it, pride or self-interest, or some rebel craving, King *de facto* of your soul, directing it back to anarchy.

For many types that, however, is exactly what happens with public worship. They *do* get a King Log in Ceremony. And if you deliberately overcome and suppress your perception of and repugnance to the perfunctoriness of religion in nine-tenths of the worshippers about you, you may be destroying at the same time your own intellectual and moral sensitiveness. But I am not suggesting that you should force yourself to take part in public worship against your perceptions, but only that if it helps you to worship you should not hesitate to do so.

We deal here with a real need that is not to be fettered by any general prescription. I have one Cambridge friend who finds nothing so uplifting in the world as the atmosphere of the afternoon service in the choir of King's College Chapel, and another, a very great and distinguished and theologically sceptical woman, who accustomed herself for some time to hear from a distant corner the evening service in St. Paul's Cathedral, and who would go great distances to do that.

Many people find an exaltation and broadening of the mind in mountain scenery and the starry heavens and the wide arc of the sea ; and, as I have already said, it was part of the disciplines of these Samurai of mine that yearly they should go apart for at least a week of solitary wandering and meditation in lonely and desolate places. Music again is a frequent means of release from the narrow life as it closes about us. One man I know makes an anthology into which he copies to re-read any passage that stirs and revives in him the sense of broad issues. Others again seem able to refresh their nobility of outlook in the atmosphere of an intense personal love.

Some of us seem to forget almost as if it were an essential part of ourselves. Such a man as myself, irritable, easily fatigued and bored, versatile, sensuous, curious, and a little greedy for experience, is perpetually losing touch with his faith, so that indeed I sometimes turn over these pages that I have written and come upon my declarations and confessions with a sense of alien surprise.

It may be, I say, that for some of us forgetting is the normal process, that one has to believe and forget and blunder and learn something and regret and suffer and so come again to belief much as we have to eat and grow hungry and eat again. What these others can get in their temples, we, after our own manner, must distil through sleepless and lonely nights, from unavoidable humiliations, from the smarting of bruised shins.

§ 12

DEMOCRACY AND ARISTOCRACY

And now having dealt with the general form of a man's duty and with his duty to himself, let me come to his attitude to his individual fellow-men.

The broad principles determining that attitude are involved in things already written in this book. The belief in a collective being gathering experience and developing will, to which every life is subordinated, renders the cruder conception of aristocracy, the idea of a select life going on amidst a majority of trivial and contemptible persons who " do not exist," untenable. It abolishes contempt. Indeed to believe at all in a comprehensive purpose in things is to abandon that attitude and all the habits and acts that imply it. But a belief in universal significance does not altogether preclude a belief in an aristocratic method of progress, in the idea of the subordination of a number of individuals to others who can utilize their lives and help and contributory achievements in the general purpose. To a certain extent, indeed, this last conception is almost inevitable. We must needs so think of ourselves in relation to plants and animals, and I see no reason why we should not think so of our relations to other men. There are clearly great differences in the capacity and range of experience of man and man and in their power of using and rendering their experiences for the racial synthesis. Vigorous persons do look naturally for help and service from persons of less initiative, and we are all more or less capable of admiration and hero-worship and pleased to help and give ourselves to those we feel to be finer or better or completer or more forceful and leaderly than ourselves. This is a natural and inevitable form of aristocracy.

For that reason aristocracy is not to be organized. We organize things that are not natural nor inevitable, but this is clearly a complex matter of accident and personalities for which there can be no general rule. All organized aristocracy is manifestly begotten by that fallacy of classification my Metaphysical book set itself to expose. Its effect is, and has been in all cases, to mask natural aristocracy, to draw the lines by wholesale and wrong, to bolster up weak and ineffectual persons in false positions, and to fetter or hamper strong and vigorous people. The false aristocrat is a figure of pride and claims, a consumer followed by dupes. He is proudly secretive, pretending to aims beyond the common understanding. The true aristocrat is known rather than knows; he makes and serves. He exacts no deference. He is urgent to make others share what he knows and wants and achieves. He does not think of others as his but as God's as he also is God's.

There is a base democracy just as there is a base
aristocracy, the swaggering, aggressive disposition
of the vulgar soul that admits neither of superiors
nor leaders.   Its true name is insubordination.   It
resents rules and refinements, delicacies, differences
and organization.   It dreams that its leaders are its
delegates.   It takes refuge from all superiority, all
special knowledge, in a phantom ideal, the People,
the sublime and wonderful People.   " You can fool
some of the people all the time and all the people
some of the time, but you can't fool all the people
all the time," expresses I think quite the quintessence
of this mystical faith, this faith in which men take
refuge from the demand for order, discipline and
conscious light.   In England it has never been of
any great account, but in America the vulgar individualist's self-protective exaltation of an idealized
Common Man has worked and is working infinite
mischief.

In politics the crude democratic faith leads directly
to the submission of every question, however subtle
and special its issues may be, to a popular vote.
The community is regarded as a consultative com-
mittee of profoundly wise, alert and well-informed
Common Men.   Since the common man is, as Gustave
le Bon has pointed out, a gregarious animal, collectively rather like a sheep, emotional, hasty and
shallow, the practical outcome of political democracy
in all large communities under modern conditions
is to put power into the hands of rich newspaper
proprietors, advertising producers and the energetic
wealthy generally who are best able to flood the
collective mind freely with the suggestions on which
it acts.

But democracy has acquired a better meaning
than its first crude intentions—there never was a
theory started yet in the human mind that did not

beget a finer offspring than itself—and the secondary meaning brings it at last into entire accordance with the subtler conception of aristocracy. The test of this quintessential democracy is neither a passionate insistence upon voting and the majority rule, nor an arrogant bearing towards those who are one's betters in this aspect or that, but fellowship. The true democrat and the true aristocrat meet and are one in feeling themselves parts of one synthesis under one purpose and one scheme. Both realize that self-concealment is the last evil, both make frankness and veracity the basis of their intercourse. The general rightness of living for you and others and for others and you is to understand them to the best of your ability and to make them all, to the utmost limits of your capacity of expression and their under-standing and sympathy, participators in your act and thought.

§ 13

ON DEBTS OF HONOUR

My ethical disposition is all against punctilio, and I set no greater value on unblemished honour than I do on purity. I never yet met a man who talked proudly of his honour who did not end by cheating or trying to cheat me, nor a code of honour that did not impress me as a conspiracy against the common welfare and purpose in life. There is honour among thieves, and I think it might well end there as an obligation in conduct. The soldier who risks a life he owes to his army in a duel upon some silly matter of personal pride is no better to me than the clerk who gambles with the money in his master's till. When I was a boy I once paid a debt of honour, and it is one of the things I am most ashamed of. I had played cards into debt and I still remember burningly how I went to my mother and got the money she could so ill afford to give me. I would not pay a debt of honour at such a price now. I would pay with my own skin or not at all. If I were to wake up one morning owing big sums that I had staked overnight I would set to work at once by every means in my power to evade and repudiate that obligation. I should be disgraced! Well and good, I should deserve it. Such money as I have I owe under our present system to wife and sons and my work and the world, and I see no valid reason why I should hand it over to Smith because he and I have played the fool and rascal and gambled. Better by far to accept that fact and be for my own part published fool and rascal than to rob these others or fall short of my tale of bricks.

I have never been able to understand the sentimental spectacle of sons toiling dreadfully and wasting themselves upon mere money-making to save the secret of a father's peculations and the " honour of the family," or men conspiring to weave a wide and mischievous net of lies to save the " honour " of a woman. In the conventional drama the preservation of the honour of a woman seems an adequate excuse for nearly any offence short of murder : the preservation, that is to say, of the appearance of something that is already gone. The honour of the family lies in every son and daughter doing his own service to the world in his own fashion. Here it is that I do definitely part company with the false aristocrat who is by nature and intent a humbug and fabricator of sham attitudes, and ally myself with democracy. Fact, valiantly faced, is of more value than any reputation. The false aristocrat is robed to the chin and unwashed beneath, the true goes stark as Apollo. The false is ridiculous with

indignified insistence upon his dignity ; the true
says like God, " I am that I am."

§ 14

THE IDEA OF JUSTICE

One word has so far played a very little part in
this book, and that is the word Justice.

Those who have read the opening book on Metaphysics will perhaps see that this is a necessary
corollary of the system of thought developed therein.
In my philosophy, with its insistence upon uniqueness and marginal differences and the provisional
nature of numbers and classes, there is little scope
for that blindfolded lady with the balances, seeking
always exact equivalents. Nowhere in my system
of thought is there work for the idea of Rights and
the conception of conscientious litigious-spirited
people exactly observing nicely defined relationships.

You will note, for example, that I base my Socialism on the idea of a collective development and not
on the " right " of every man to his own labour, or
his " right " to work, or his " right " to subsistence.
All these ideas of " rights " and of a social " contract,"
however implicit, are merely conventional ways of
looking at things, conventions that have arisen in
the mercantile phase of human development.

Laws and rights, like common terms in speech,
are provisional things, conveniences for taking hold
of a number of cases that would otherwise be un-
manageable. The appeal to Justice is a necessarily
inadequate attempt to de-individualize a case, to
eliminate the self's biased attitude. I have declared
that it is my wilful belief that everything that exists
is significant and necessary. The idea of Justice

seems to me a defective, quantitative application of the spirit of that belief to men and women. In every case you try and discover and act upon a plausible equity that must necessarily be based on arbitrary assumptions.

There is no equity in the universe, in the various spectacle outside our minds, and the most terrible nightmare the human imagination has ever engendered is a Just God, measuring, with Himself as the Standard, against finite men. Ultimately there is no adequacy, we are all weighed in the balance and found wanting.

So, as the recognition of this has grown, Justice has been tempered with Mercy, which indeed is no more than an attempt to equalize things by making the factors of the very defect that is condemned, its condonation. The modern mind fluctuates uncertainly somewhere between these extremes, now harsh and now ineffectual.

To me there seems no validity in these quasi-absolute standards.

A man seeks and obeys standards of equity simply to economize his moral effort, not because there is anything true or sublime about justice, but because he knows he is too egoistic and weak-minded and obsessed to do any perfect thing at all, because he cannot trust himself with his own transitory emotions unless he trains himself beforehand to observe a predetermined rule. There is scarcely an eventuality in life that without the help of these generalizations would not exceed the average man's intellectual power and moral energy, just as there is scarcely an idea or an emotion that can be conveyed without the use of faulty and defective common names. Justice and Mercy are indeed not ultimately different in their nature from such other conventions as the rules of a game, the rules of etiquette, forms of address, cab tariffs, and standards of all sorts. They are mere organizations of relationship either to economize thought or else to facilitate mutual understanding and codify common action. Modesty and self-submission, love and service, are, in the system of my beliefs, far more fundamental rightnesses and duties.

We are not mercantile and litigious units such as making Justice our social basis would imply, we are not select responsible right persons mixed with and tending weak irresponsible wrong persons such as the notion of Mercy suggests; we are parts of one being and body, each unique yet sharing a common nature and a variety of imperfections and working together (albeit more or less darkly and ignorantly) for a common end.

We are strong and weak together and in one brotherhood. The weak have no essential rights against the strong, nor the strong against the weak. The world does not exist for our weaknesses but our strength. And the real justification of democracy lies in the fact that none of us are altogether strong nor altogether weak; for everyone there is an aspect wherein he is seen to be weak; for everyone there is a strength though it may be only a little peculiar strength or an undeveloped potentiality. The unconverted man uses his strength egotistically, emphasizes himself harshly against the man who is weak where he is strong, and hates and conceals his own weakness. The Believer, in the measure of his belief, respects and seeks to understand the different strength of others and to use his own distinctive power with and not against his fellow-men, in the common service of that synthesis to which each one of them is ultimately as necessary as he.

§ 15

OF LOVE AND JUSTICE

Now here the friend who has read the first dra′t
of this book falls into something like a dispute with
me. She does not, I think, like this dismissal of
Justice from a primary place in my scheme of conduct.

"Justice," she asserts, "is an instinctive craving
very nearly akin to the physical craving for equilib-
rium. Its social importance corresponds. It seeks
to keep the individual's claims in such a position as
to conflict as little as possible with those of others.
Justice is the root instinct of all social feeling, of all
feeling which does not take account of whether we
like or dislike individuals; it is the feeling of an
orderly position of our Ego towards others, merely
considered *as* others, and of all the Egos merely *as*
Egos towards each other. *Love* cannot be felt towards
others *as* others. Love is the expression of individual
suitability and preference, its positive existence in
some cases implies its absolute negation in others.
Hence Love can never be the essential and root of
social feeling, and hence the necessity for the instinct
of abstract justice which takes no account of preferences or aversions. And here I may say that all
application of the word *love* to unknown, distant
creatures, to mere *others*, is a perversion and a wasting
of the word love, which, taking its origin in sexual
and parental preference, always implies a preference
of one object to the other. To love everybody is
simply not to love at all. And it is *just because* of
the passionate preference instinctively felt for some
individuals that mankind requires the self-regarding
and self-respecting passion of justice."

Now this is not altogether contradictory of what
I hold. I disagree that because love necessarily

expresses itself in preference, selecting this rather than that, that it follows necessarily that its absolute negation is implied in the non-selected cases. A man may go into the world as a child goes into a garden and gathers its hands full of the flowers that please it best and then desists, but only because its hands are full and not because it is at an end of the flowers that it can find delight in. So the man finds at last his memory and apprehensions glutted. It is not that he could not love those others. And I dispute that to love everybody is not to love at all. To love two people is surely to love more than to love just one person, and so by way of three and four to a very large number. Love is not an individual thing merely. One may love a class. I love the cheerful English soldier. I love smiling people. But if it is put that love must be a preference because of the mental limitations that forbid us to apprehend and understand more than a few of the multitudinous lovables of life, then I agree. For all the individuals and things and cases for which we have inadequate time and energy, we need a wholesale method—justice. That is exactly what I have said in the previous section. Justice is a time- and energy-saving device : nothing more.

§ 16

THE WEAKNESS OF IMMATURITY

One is apt to write and talk of strong and weak as though some were always strong, some always weak. But that is quite a misleading version of life. Apart from the fact that everyone is fluctuatingly strong and fluctuatingly weak, and weak and strong according to the quality we judge them by, we have to remember that we are all developing and learning and changing, gaining strength and at last losing it, from the cradle to the grave. We are all, to borrow the old scholastic term, pupil-teachers of Life ; the term is none the less appropriate because the pupil-teacher taught badly and learned under difficulties.

It may seem to be a crowning feat of platitude to write that " we have to remember " this, but it is overlooked in a whole mass of legal, social and economic literature. Those extraordinary imaginary cases as between a man A and a man B who start level, on a desert island or elsewhere, and work or do not work, or save or do not save, become the basis of immense schemes of just arrangement which soar up confidently and serenely regardless of the fact that never did anything like that equal start occur ; that from the beginning there were family groups and old heads and young heads, help, guidance and sacrifice, and those who had learned and those who had still to learn, jumbled together in confused transactions. Deals, tradings and so forth are entirely secondary aspects of these primaries, and the attempt to get an idea of abstract relationship by beginning upon a secondary issue is the fatal pervading fallacy in all these regions of thought. At the present moment the average age of the world is, I suppose, about 21 or 22, the normal death somewhen about 44 or 45, that is to say nearly half the world is " under age," green, inexperienced, demanding help, easily misled and put in the wrong and betrayed. Yet the younger moiety, if we do indeed assume life's object is a collective synthesis, is more important than the older, and every older person bound to be something of a guardian to the younger. It follows directly from the fundamental beliefs I have assumed that we are missing the most important aspects of life if we are not directly or indirectly serving the young, helping them individually or collectively. Just in the measure that one's living falls away from that, do we fall away from life into a mere futility of existence, and approach the state, the extraordinary and wonderful middle state of (for example) those extinct and entirely damned old gentlemen one sees and hears eating and sleeping in every comfortable London club.

§ 17

POSSIBILITY OF A NEW ETIQUETTE

These two ideas, firstly the pupil-teacher parental idea and secondly the democratic idea (that is to say, the idea of an equal ultimate significance), the second correcting any tendency in the first to pedagogic arrogance and tactful concealments, do I think give, when taken together, the general attitude a right-living man will take to his individual fellow-creature. They play against each other, providing elements of contradiction and determining a balanced course. It seems to me to follow necessarily from my fundamental beliefs that the Believer will tend to be and want to be and seek to be friendly to, and interested in, all sorts of people, and truthful and helpful and hating concealment. To be that with any approach to perfection demands an intricate and difficult effort, introspection to the hilt of one's power, a saving natural gift ; one has to avoid pedantry, aggression, brutality, amiable - tiresomeness—there are pitfalls on every side. The more one thinks about other people the more interesting and pleasing they are ; I am all for kindly gossip and knowing things about them, and all against the silly and limiting hardness of soul that will not look into one's fellows nor go out to them. The use and justification of most literature, of fiction, verse, history, biography, is that it lets us into understandings and the suggestion of human

E

possibilities. The general purpose of intercourse is to get as close as one can to the realities of the people one meets, and to give oneself to them just so far as possible.

From that I think there arises naturally a new etiquette that would set aside many of the rigidities of procedure that keep people apart to-day. There is a fading prejudice against asking personal questions, against talking about oneself or one's immediate personal interests, against discussing religion and politics and any such keenly felt matter. No doubt it is necessary at times to protect oneself against clumsy and stupid familiarities, against noisy and inattentive egotists, against intriguers and liars, but only in the last resort do such breaches of patience seem justifiable to me; for the most part our traditions of speech and intercourse altogether overdo separations, the preservation of distances and protective devices in general.

§ 18

SEX

So far as I have ignored the immense importance of Sex in our lives and for the most part kept the discussion so generalized as to apply impartially to women and men. But now I have reached a point when this great boundary line between two halves of the world and the intense and intimate personal problems that play across it must be considered.

For not only must we bend our general activities and our intellectual life to the conception of a human synthesis, but out of our bodies and emotional possibilities we have to make the new world bodily and emotionally. To the test of that we have to bring all sorts of questions that agitate us to-day, the social and political equality and personal freedom of women, the differing code of honour for the sexes, the controls and limitations to set upon love and desire. If, for example, it is for the good of the species that a whole half of its individuals should be specialized and sub-ordinated to the physical sexual life, as in certain phases of human development women have tended to be, then certainly we must do nothing to prevent that. We have set aside the conception of Justice as in any sense a countervailing idea to that of the synthetic process.

And it is well to remember that for the whole of sexual conduct that is quite conceivably no general simple rule. It is quite possible that, as Metchnikoff maintains in his extraordinarily illuminating *Nature of Man*, we are dealing with an irresolvable tangle of disharmonies. We have passions that do not insist upon their physiological end, desires that may be prematurely vivid in childhood, a fantastic curiosity, old needs of the ape but thinly overlaid by the acqui-sitions of the man, emotions that jar with physical impulses, inexplicable pains and diseases. And not only have we to remember that we are dealing with disharmonies that may at the very best be only patched together, but we are dealing with matters in which the element of idiosyncrasy is essential, insist-ing upon an incalculable flexibility in any rule we make, unless we are to take types and indeed whole classes of personality and write them down as abso-lutely bad and fit only for suppression and restraint. And on the mental side we are further perplexed by the extraordinary suggestibility of human beings. In sexual matters there seems to me—and I think I share a general ignorance here—to be no directing instinct at all, but only an instinct to do something generally sexual ; there are almost equally powerful desires to do right and not to act under compulsion.

The specific forms of conduct imposed upon these instincts and desires depend upon a vast confusion of suggestions, institutions, conventions, ways of putting things. We are dealing therefore with problems ineradicably complex, varying endlessly in their instances, and changing as we deal with them. I am inclined to think that the only really profitable discussion of sexual matters is in terms of individuality, through the novel, the lyric, the play, autobiography or biography of the frankest sort. But such generalizations as I can make I will.

To me it seems manifest that sexual matters may be discussed generally in at least three permissible and valid ways, of which the consideration of the world as a system of births and education is only the dominant chief. There is next the question of the physical health and beauty of the community and how far sexual rules and customs affect that, and thirdly the question of the mental and moral atmosphere in which sexual conventions and laws must necessarily be an important factor. It is alleged that probably in the case of men, and certainly in the case of women, some sexual intercourse is a necessary phase in existence ; that without it there is an incompleteness, a failure in the life cycle, a real wilting and failure of energy and vitality and the development of morbid states. And for most of us half the friendships and intimacies from which we derive the daily interest and sustaining force in our lives draw mysterious elements from sexual attraction, and depend and hesitate upon our conception of the liberties and limits we must give to that force.

§ 19

THE INSTITUTION OF MARRIAGE

The individual attitudes of men to women and of women to men are necessarily determined to a large extent by certain general ideas of relationship, by institutions and conventions. One of the most important and debatable of these is whether we are to consider and treat women as citizens and fellows, or as beings differing mentally from men and grouped in positions of at least material dependence to individual men. Our decision in that direction will affect all our conduct from the larger matters down to the smallest points of deportment ; it will affect even our manner of address and determine whether when we speak to a woman we shall be as frank and unaffected as with a man or touched with a faint suggestion of the reserves of a cat which does not wish to be suspected of wanting to steal the milk.

Now so far as that goes it follows almost necessarily from my views upon aristocracy and democracy that I declare for the conventional equality of women, that is to say for the determination to make neither sex nor any sexual characteristic a standard of superiority or inferiority, for the view that a woman is a person as important and necessary, as much to be consulted, and entitled to as much freedom of action as a man.   I admit that this decision is a choice into which temperament enters, that I cannot produce compelling reasons why anyone else should adopt my view. I can produce considerations in support of my view, that is all. But they are so implicit in all that has gone before that I will not trouble to detail them here.

The conception of equality and fellowship between men and women is an idea at least as old as Plato and one that has recurred wherever civilization has reached a phase in which men and women were sufficiently released from militant and economic urgency to talk and read and think. But it has never yet been, at least in the historical period and in any but isolated social groups, a working structural idea. The working structural idea is the Patriarchal Family in which the woman is inferior and submits herself and is subordinated to the man, the head of the family.

We live in a constantly changing development and modification of that tradition. It is well to bring that factor of constant change into mind at the outset of this discussion and to keep it there. To forget it, and it is commonly forgotten, is to falsify every issue. Marriage and the Family are perennially fluctuating institutions, and probably scarcely anything in modern life has changed and is changing so much ; they are in their legal constitution or their moral and emotional quality profoundly different things from what they were a hundred years ago. A woman who marries nowadays marries, if one may put it quantitatively, far less than she did even half a century ago ; the Married Woman's Property Act, for example, has revolutionized the economic relationship ; her husband has lost his right to assault her, and he cannot even compel her to cohabit with him if she refuses to do so. Legal separations and divorces have come to modify the quality and logical consequences of the bond. The rights of parent over the child have been even more completely qualified. The State has come in as protector and educator of the children, taking over personal powers and responsibilities that have been essential to the family institution ever since the dawn of history. It inserts itself more and more between child and parent. It invades what were once the most sacred intimacies, and the

Salvation Army is now promoting legislation to explore those overcrowded homes in which children (it is estimated to the number of thirty or forty thousand) are living, as I write, daily witnesses of their mother's prostitution or in constant danger of incestuous attack from drunken fathers and brothers. And finally as another indication of profound differences, births were almost universally accidental a hundred years ago ; they are now in an increasing number of families controlled and deliberate acts of will. In every one of their relations do Marriage and the Family change and continue to change.

But the inherent defectiveness of the human mind which my metaphysical book sets itself to analyse does lead it constantly to speak of Marriage and the Family as things as fixed and unalterable as, let us say, the characteristics of oxygen. One is asked, Do you believe in Marriage and the Family ? as if it was a case of either having or not having some definite thing. Socialists are accused of being " against the Family," as if it were not the case that Socialists, Individualists, High Anglicans and Roman Catholics are *all* against Marriage and the Family as these institutions exist at the present time. But once we have realized the absurdity of this absolute treatment, then it should become clear that with it goes most of the fabric of right and wrong, and nearly all those arbitrary standards by which we classify people into moral and immoral. Those last words are used when as a matter of fact we mean either conforming or failing to conform to changing laws and developing institutional customs we may or may not consider right or wrong. Their use imparts a flavour of essential wrong-doing and obliquity into acts and relations that may be in many cases no more than social indiscipline, which may be even conceivably a courageous act of defiance to an obsolescent limitation. Such, until a little while ago, was a man's co-habitation with his deceased wife's sister. This, which was scandalous yesterday, is now a legally honourable relationship, albeit I believe still regarded by the High Anglican as incestuous wickedness.

I am persuaded of the need of much greater facilities of divorce than exist at present, divorce on the score of mutual consent, of faithlessness, of simple cruelty, of insanity, habitual vice, or the prolonged imprisonment of either party. And this being so I find it impossible to condemn on any ground, except that it is " breaking ranks " and making a confusion, those who by anticipating such wide facilities as I propose have sinned by existing standards. How far and in what manner such breaking of ranks is to be condoned I will presently discuss. But it is clear it is an offence of a different nature from actions one believes to be in themselves and apart from the law reprehensible things.

But my scepticisms about the current legal institutions and customary code are not exhausted by these modifications I have suggested. I believe firmly in some sort of marriage, that is to say, an open declaration of the existence of sexual relations between a man and a woman, because I am averse to all unnecessary secrecies and because the existence of these peculiarly intimate relationships affects everybody about the persons concerned. It is ridiculous to say as some do that sexual relations between two people affect no one but themselves unless a child is born. They do, because they tend to break down barriers and set up a peculiar emotional partnership. It is a partnership that kept secret may work as antisocially as a secret business partnership or a secret preferential railway tariff. And I believe too in the general social desirability of the family group, the normal group of father, mother and children, and in the extreme efficacy in the normal human being of the blood link and pride link between parent and child in securing loving care and upbringing for the child. But this clear adhesion to Marriage and to the family grouping about mother and father does not close the door to a large series of exceptional cases which our existing institutions and customs ignore or crush.

For example, monogamy in general seems to me to be clearly indicated (as doctors say) by the fact that there are not several women in the world for every man, but quite as clearly does it seem necessary to recognize that the fact that there are (or were in 1901) 21,436,107 females to 20,172,984 males in our British community seems to condemn our present rigorous insistence upon monogamy, unless feminine celibacy has its own delights. But, as I have said, it is now largely believed that the sexual life of a woman is more important to her than his sexual life to a man and less easily ignored.

It is true also cn the former side, that for the great majority of people one knows personally, any sort of household but a monogamous one conjures up painful and unpleasant visions. The ordinary civilized woman and the ordinary civilized man are alike obsessed with the idea of meeting and possessing one peculiar intimate person, one special exclusive lover who is their very own, and a third person of either sex cannot be associated with that couple without an intolerable sense of privacy and confidence and possession destroyed. But if there are people so exceptionally constituted as not to feel in this way, I do not see what right we have to force conformity to our feelings upon them.

The peculiar defects of the human mind when they approach these questions of sex are reinforced by passions peculiar to the topic, and it is perhaps advisable to point out that to discuss these possibilities is not the same thing as to urge the reader to hazardous experiments. We are trained from the nursery to become secretive, muddle-headed and vehemently conclusive upon sexual matters, until at last the editors of magazines blush at the very phrase and long to put a petticoat over the page that bears it. Yet our rebellious natures insist on being interested by it. It seems to me that to judge these large questions from the personal point of view, to insist upon the whole world without exception living exactly in the manner that suits oneself or accords with one's emotional imagination and the forms of delicacy in which one has been trained, is not the proper way to deal with them. I want as a sane social organizer to get just as many contented and law-abiding citizens as possible ; I do not want to force people who would otherwise be useful citizens into rebellion, concealments and the dark and furtive ways of vice, because they may not love and marry as their temperaments command, and so I want to make the meshes of the law as wide as possible. But the common man will not understand this yet, and seeks to make the meshes just as small as his own private case demands.

Then marriage, to resume my main discussion, does not necessarily mean cohabitation. All women who desire children do not want to be entrusted with their upbringing. Some women are sexual and philoprogenitive without being sedulously maternal, and some are maternal without much or any sexual passion. There are men and women in the world now, great allies, fond and passionate lovers who do not live nor want to live constantly together. It is at least conceivable that there are women who, while desiring offspring, do not want to abandon great careers for the work of maternity, women again who would be happiest managing and rearing children in manless households that they might even share with other women friends, and men to correspond with these who do not wish to live in a household with wife and children. I submit, these temperaments exist and have a right to exist in their own way. But one must recognize that the possibility of these departures from the normal type of household opens up other possibilities. The polygamy that is degrading or absurd under one roof assumes a different appearance when one considers it from the point of view of people whose habits of life do not centre upon an isolated home.

All the relations I have glanced at above do as a matter of fact exist to-day, but shamefully and shabbily, tainted with what seems to me an unmerited and unnecessary ignominy and frequently darkened by blackmail. A narrow, intolerant community is the blackmailer's paradise. The punishment for bigamy, again, seems to me insane in its severity, contrasted as it is with our leniency to the common seducer. Better ruin a score of women, says the law, than marry two. I do not see why in these matters there should not be much ampler freedom than there is, and this being so I can hardly be expected to condemn with any moral fervour or exclude from my society those who have seen fit to behave by what I believe may be the standards of A.D. 2000 instead of by the standards of 1850. These are offences, so far as they are offences, on an altogether different footing from murder, or exacting usury, or the sweating of children, or cruelty, or transmitting diseases, or unveracity, or commercial or intellectual or physical prostitution, or any such essentially grave anti-social deeds. We must distinguish between sins on the one hand and mere errors of judgment and differences of taste from ourselves. To draw up harsh laws, to practise exclusions against everyone who does not see fit to duplicate one's own blameless home life, is to waste a number of courageous and exceptional persons in every generation, to drive many of them into a forced alliance with real crime and embittered rebellion against custom and the law.

§ 20

CONDUCT IN RELATION TO THE THING THAT IS

But the reader must keep clear in his mind the distinction between conduct that is right or permissible in itself and conduct that becomes either inadvisable or mischievous and wrong because of the circumstances about it. There is no harm under ordinary conditions in asking a boy with a pleasant voice to sing a song in the night, but the case is altered altogether if you have reason to suppose that a Red Indian is lying in wait a hundred yards off, holding a loaded rifle and ready to fire at the voice. It is a valid objection to many actions that I do not think objectionable in themselves, that to do them will discharge a loaded prejudice into the heart of my friend—or even into my own. I belong to the world and my work, and I must not lightly throw my time, my power, my influence away. For a splendid thing any risk or any defiance may be justifiable, but is it a sufficiently splendid thing? So far as he possibly can a man must conform to common prejudices, prevalent customs and all laws, whatever his estimate of them may be. But he must at the same time do his utmost to change what he thinks to be wrong.

And I think that conformity must be honest conformity. There is no more anti-social act than secret breaches, and only some very urgent and exceptional occasion justifies even the unveracity of silence about the thing done. If your personal convictions bring

you to a breach, let it be an open breach, let there be
no misrepresentation of attitudes, no meanness, no
deception of honourable friends.   Of course an open
breach need not be an ostentatious breach ; to do
what is right to yourself without fraud or concealment is one thing, to make a challenge and aggression quite another.   Your friends may understand
and sympathize and condone, but it does not lie upon
you to force them to identify themselves with your
act and situation.   But better too much openness
than too little.   Squalid intrigue was the shadow of
the old intolerably narrow order ; it is a shadow we
want to illuminate out of existence.   Secrets will
be contraband in the new time.

And if it chances to you to feel called upon to
make a breach with the institution or custom or
prejudice that is, remember that doing so is your
own affair.   You are going to take risks and specialize
as an experiment.   You must not expect other
people about you to share the consequences of your
dash forward.   You must not drag in confidants and
secondaries.   You must fight your little battle in
front on your own responsibility, unsupported—and
take the consequences without repining.

§ 21

CONDUCT TOWARDS TRANSGRESSORS

So far as breaches of the prohibitions and laws of
marriage go, to me it seems they are to be tolerated
by us in others just in the measure that, within the
limits set by discretion, they are frank and truthful
and animated by spontaneous passion and pervaded
by the quality of beauty.   I hate the vulgar sexual
intriguer, man or woman, and the smart and shallow
atmosphere of unloving lust and vanity about the

type as I hate few kinds of human life ; I would as lief have a polecat in my home as this sort of person ; and every sort of prostitute except the victim of utter necessity I despise, even though marriage be the fee. But honest lovers should be, I think, a charge and pleasure for us.   We must judge each pair as we can.

One thing renders a sexual relationship incurably offensive to others and altogether wrong, and that is cruelty.   But who can define cruelty ?   How far is the leaving of a third person to count as cruelty ?   There again I hesitate to judge.   To love and not be loved is a fate for which it seems no one can be blamed ; to lose love and to change one's loving belongs to a subtle interplay beyond analysis or control, but to be deceived or mocked or deliberately robbed of love, that at any rate is an abominable wrong.

In all these matters I perceive a general rule is in itself a possible instrument of cruelty.   I set down what I can in the way of general principles, but it all leaves off far short of the point of application.   Every case among those we know I think we moderns must judge for ourselves.   Where there is doubt, there I hold must be charity.   And with regard to strangers, manifestly our duty is to avoid inquisitorial and un-charitable acts.

This is as true of financial and economic miscon-duct as of sexual misconduct, of ways of living that are socially harmful and of political faith.   We are dealing with people in a maladjusted world to whom absolute right living is practically impossible, because there are no absolutely right institutions and no simple choice of good or evil, and we have to balance merits and defects in every case.

Some people are manifestly and essentially base and self-seeking and regardless of the happiness and welfare of their fellows, some in business affairs and politics as others in love.   Some wrong-doers, again, are evidently so through heedlessness, through weakness, timidity or haste. We have to judge and deal with each sort upon no clear issue, but upon impressions they have given us of their spirit and purpose. We owe it to them and ourselves not to judge too rashly or too harshly, but for all that we are obliged to judge and take sides, to avoid the malignant and exclude them for further opportunity, to help and champion the cheated and the betrayed, to forgive and aid the repentant blunderer, and by mercy to save the lesser sinner from desperate alliance with the greater. That is the broad rule, and it is as much as we have to go upon until the individual case comes before us.

BOOK THE FOURTH

SOME PERSONAL THINGS

§ 1

PERSONAL LOVE AND LIFE

It has been most convenient to discuss all that might
be generalized about conduct first, to put in the
common background the vistas and atmosphere of
the scene.   But a man's relations are of two orders,
and these questions of rule and principle are over
and about and round more vivid and immediate interests.   A man is not simply a relationship between
his individual self and the race, society and the world.
Close about him are persons, friends and enemies and
lovers and beloved people.   He desires them, lusts
after them, craves their affection, needs their presence, abhors them, hates and desires to limit and
suppress them.   This is for most of us the flesh and
blood of life.   We go through the scene of the world
neither alone, nor alone with God, nor serving an
undistinguishable multitude, but in a company of
individualized people.

Here is a system of motives and passions, imperious
and powerful, which follows no broad general rule
and in which each man must needs be a light unto
himself upon innumerable issues.   I am satisfied that
these personal urgencies are neither to be suppressed
nor crudely nor ruthlessly subordinated to the general
issues.   Religious and moral teachers are apt to
make this part of life either too detached or too

insignificant. They teach it either as if it did not matter or as if it ought not to matter. Indeed our individual friends and enemies stand between us and hide or interpret for us all the larger things. Few can even worship alone. They must feel others, and those not strangers, kneeling beside them.

I have already spoken under the heading of Beliefs of the part that the idea of a Mediator has played and can play in the religious life. I have pointed out how the imagination of men has sought and found in certain personalities, historical or fictitious, a bridge between the blood-warm private life and the intolerable spaciousness of right and wrong. The world is full of such figures and their images, Christ and Mary and the Saints, and all the lesser, dearer gods of heathendom. These things and the human passion for living leaders and heroes and leagues and brotherhoods all confess the mediatory rôle, the mediatory possibilities of personal love between the individual and the great synthesis of which he is a part and agent. The great synthesis may become incarnate in personal love, and personal love lead us directly to universal service.

I write *may*, and temper that sentence to the quality of a possibility alone. This is true only for those who believe, for those who have faith, whose lives have been unified, who have found Salvation. For those whose lives are chaotic, personal loves must also be chaotic; this or that passion, malice, a jesting humour, some physical lust, gratified vanity, egotistical pride, will rule and limit the relationship and colour its ultimate futility. But the Believer uses personal love and sustains himself by personal love. It is his provender, the meat and drink of his campaign.

§ 2

THE NATURE OF LOVE

It is well perhaps to look a little into the factors that make up Love.

Love does not seem to me to be a simple elemental thing. It is, as I have already said, one of the vicious tendencies of the human mind to think that whatever can be given a simple name can be abstracted as a single something in a state of quintessential purity. I have pointed out that this is not true of Harmony or Beauty, and that these are synthetic things. You bring together this which is not beautiful and that which is not beautiful, and behold! Beauty! So also Love is, I think, a synthetic thing. One observes this and that, one is interested and stirred; suddenly the metal fuses, the dry bones live! One loves.

Almost every interest in one's being may be a factor in the love synthesis. But apart from the overflowing of the parental instinct that makes all that is fine and delicate and young dear to us and to be cherished, there are two main factors that bring us into love with our fellows. There are first the emotional elements in our nature that arise out of the tribal necessity, out of a fellowship in battle and hunting, drinking and feasting, out of the needs and excitements and delights of those occupations; and there are next the intenser narrower desirings and gratitudes, satisfactions and expectations that come from sexual intercourse. Now both these factors originate in physical needs and consummate in material acts, and it is well to remember that this great growth of love in life roots there, and, it may be, dies when its roots are altogether cut away.

At its lowest, love is the mere sharing of, or rather the desire to share, pleasure and excitement, the excitements of conflict or lust or what not. I think that the desire to partake, the desire to merge one's individual identity with another's, remains a necessary element in all personal loves. It is a way out of ourselves, a breaking down of our individual separation, just as hate is an intensification of that. Personal love is the narrow and intense form of that breaking down, just as what I call Salvation is its widest, most extensive form. We cast aside our reserves, our secrecies, our defences; we open ourselves; touches that would be intolerable from common people become a mystery of delight, acts of self-abasement and self-sacrifice are charged with symbolical pleasure. We cannot tell which of us is me, which you. Our imprisoned egoism looks out through this window, forgets its walls, and is for those brief moments released and universal.

For most of us the strain of primordial sexual emotion in our loves is very strong. Many men can love only women, many women only men, and some can scarcely love at all without bodily desire. But the love of fellowship is a strong one also, and for many, love is most possible and easy when the thought of physical love-making has been banished. Then the lovers will pursue other interests together, will work together or journey together. So we have the warm fellowships of men for men and women for women. But even then it may happen that men friends together will talk of women, and women friends of men. Nevertheless we have also the strong and altogether sexless glow of those who have fought well together, or drunk or jested together or hunted a common quarry.

Now it seems to me that the Believer must also be a Lover, that he will love as much as he can and as many people as he can, and in many moods and ways. As I have said already, many of those who

have taught religion and morality in the past have
been neglectful or unduly jealous of the intenser personal loves. They have been, to put it by a figure,
urgent upon the road to the ocean. To that they
would lead us, though we come to it shivering, fear-
ful and unprepared, and they grudge it that we
should strip and plunge into the wayside stream.
But all streams, all rivers come from this ocean in
the beginning, lead to it in the end.

It is the essential fact of love, as I conceive it,
that it breaks down the boundaries of self. That
love is most perfect which does most completely
merge its lovers. But no love is altogether perfect,
and for most men and women love is no more than a
partial and temporary lowering of the barriers that
keep them apart. With many, the attraction of love
seems always to fall short of what I hold to be its
end, it draws people together in the most momentary
of self-forgetfulnesses, and for the rest seems rather
to enhance their egotisms and their difference. They
are secret from one another even in their embraces.
There is a sort of love that is egotistical lust almost
regardless of its partner, a sort of love that is mere
fleshless pride and vanity at a white heat. There is
the love-making that springs from sheer boredom,
like a man reading a story-book to fill an hour. These
inferior loves seek to accomplish an agreeable act, or
they seek the pursuit or glory of a living possession,
they aim at gratification or excitement or conquest.
True love seeks to be mutual and easy-minded, free
of doubts, but these egotistical mockeries of love
have always resentment in them and hatred in them
and a watchful distrust. Jealousy is the measure of
self-love in love.

True love is a synthetic thing, an outcome of life,
it is not a universal thing. It is the individualized
correlative of Salvation ; like that it is a synthetic

consequence of conflicts and confusions. Many people do not desire or need Salvation, they cannot understand it, much less achieve it ; for them chaotic life suffices. So, too, many never, save for some rare moment of illumination, desire or feel love. Its happy abandonment, its careless self-giving, these things are mere foolishness to them. But much has been said and sung of faith and love alike, and in their confused greed these things also they desire and parody. So they act worship and make a fine fuss of their devotions. And also they must have a few half-furtive, half-flaunting fallen love-triumphs prowling the secret back-streets of their lives, they know not why.

(In setting this down be it remembered I am doing my best to tell what is in me because I am trying to put my whole view of life before the reader without any vital omissions. These are difficult matters to explain because they have no clear outlines ; one lets in a hard light suddenly upon things that have lurked in warm intimate shadows, dim inner things engendering motives. I am not only telling quasi-secret things but exploring them for myself. They are none the less real and important because they are elusive.)

True love I think is not simply felt but known. Just as Salvation, as I conceive it, demands a fine intelligence and mental activity, so love calls to brain and body alike and all one's powers. There is always elaborate thinking and dreaming in love. Love will stir imaginations that have never stirred before.

Love may be, and is for the most part, one-sided. It is the going out from oneself that is love, and not the accident of its return. It is the expedition whether it fail or succeed.

But an expedition starves that comes to no port.

Love always seeks mutuality and grows by the sense of responses, or we should love beautiful inanimate things more passionately than we do. Failing a full return it makes the most of an inadequate return. Failing a sustained return it welcomes a temporary coincidence. Failing a return it finds support in accepted sacrifices. But it seeks a full return, and the fullness of life has come only to those who, loving, have met the lover.

I am trying to be as explicit as possible in thus writing about Love. But the substance in which one works here is emotion that evades definition; poetic flashes and figures of speech are truer than prosaic statements. Body and the most sublimated ecstasy pass into one another, exchange themselves and elude every net of words we cast.

I have put out two ideas of unification and self-devotion, extremes upon a scale one from another; one of these ideas is that devotion to the Purpose in things I have called Salvation; the other that devotion to some other most fitting and satisfying individual which is passionate love, the former extensive as the universe, the latter the intensest thing in life. These, it seems to me, are the boundary and the living capital of the empire of life we rule.

All empires need a comprehending boundary, but many have not one capital but many chief cities, and all have cities and towns and villages beyond the capital. It is an impoverished capital that has no dependent towns, and it is a poor love that will not overflow in affection and eager kindly curiosity and sympathy and the search for fresh mutuality. To love is to go living radiantly through the world. To love and be loved is to be fearless of experience and rich in the power to give.

§ 3

THE WILL TO LOVE

Love is a thing to a large extent in its beginnings voluntary and controllable, and at last quite involuntary. It is so hedged about by obligations and consequences, real and artificial, that for the most part I think people are overmuch afraid of it. And also the tradition of sentiment that suggests its forms and guides it in the world about us is far too strongly exclusive. It is not so much when love is glowing as when it is becoming habitual that it is jealous for itself and others. Lovers a little exhausting their mutual interest find a fillip in an alliance against the world. They bury their talent of understanding and sympathy to return it duly in a clean napkin. They narrow their interest in life lest the other lover should misunderstand their amplitude as disloyalty.

Our institutions and social customs seem all to assume a definiteness of preference, a singleness and a limitation of love, which is not psychologically justifiable. People do not, I think, fall naturally into agreement with these assumptions ; they train themselves to agreement. They take refuge from experiences that seem to carry with them the risk at least of perplexing situations, in a theory of barred possibilities and locked doors. How far this shy and cultivated irresponsive lovelessness towards the world at large may not carry with it the possibility of compensating intensities, I do not know. Quite equally probable is a starvation of one's emotional nature.

The same reasons that make me decided against mere wanton abstinences make me hostile to the common convention of emotional indifference to most of the charming and interesting people one encounters. In pleasing and being pleased, in the mutual interest, the mutual opening out of people to one another, is the key of the door to all sweet and mellow living.

§ 4

LOVE AND DEATH

For him who has faith, death, so far as it is his own death, ceases to possess any quality of terror. The experiment will be over, the rinsed beaker returned to its shelf, the crystals gone dissolving down the waste-pipe ; the duster sweeps the bench. But the deaths of those we love are harder to understand or bear.

It happens that of those very intimate with me I have lost only one, and that came slowly and elaborately, a long gradual separation wrought by the accumulation of years and mental decay, but many close friends and many whom I have counted upon for sympathy and fellowship have passed out of my world. I miss such a one as Bob Stevenson, that luminous, extravagant talker, that eager fantastic mind. I miss him whenever I write. It is less pleasure now to write a story since he will never read it, much less give me a word of praise for it. And I miss York Powell's friendly laughter and Henley's exuberant welcome. They made a warmth that has gone, those men. I can understand why I, with my fumbling lucidities and explanations, have to finish up presently and go, expressing as I do the mood of a type and of a time ; but not those radiant presences.

And the gap these men have left, these men with whom after all I only sat now and again, or wrote to in a cheerful mood or got a letter from at odd times, gives me some measure of the thing that happens, that may happen, when the mind that is always near one's thoughts, the person who moves to one's movement and lights nearly all the common flow of events about one with the reminder of fellowship and meaning—ceases.

Faith which feeds on personal love must at last prevail over it. If Faith has any virtue it must have it here when we find ourselves bereft and isolated, facing a world from which the light has fled leaving it bleak and strange. We live for experience and the race; these individual interludes are just helps to that; the warm inn in which we lovers met and refreshed was but a halt on a journey. When we have loved to the intensest point we have done our best with each other. To keep to that image of the inn, we must not sit overlong at our wine beside the fire. We must go on to new experiences and new adventures. Death comes to part us and turn us out and set us on the road again.

But the dead stay where we leave them.

I suppose that is the real good in death, that they do stay; that it makes them immortal for us. Living they were mortal. But now they can never spoil themselves or be spoiled by change again. They have finished—for us indeed just as much as themselves. There they sit for ever, rounded off and bright and done. Beside these clear and certain memories I have of my dead, my impressions of the living are vague provisional things.

And since they are gone out of the world and become immortal memories in me, I feel no need to think of them as in some disembodied and incomprehensible elsewhere, changed and yet not done. I want actual immortality for those I love as little as I desire it for myself.

Indeed I dislike the idea that those I have loved are immortal in any real sense; it conjures up dim uncomfortable drifting phantoms, that have no kindred with the flesh and blood I knew. I would as

soon think of them trailing after the tides up and
down the Channel outside my window. Bob Stevenson for me is a presence utterly concrete, slouching,
eager, quick-eyed, intimate and profound, carelessly
dressed (at Sandgate he commonly wore a felt hat
that belonged to his little son) and himself, himself,
indissoluble matter and spirit, down to the heels of
his boots. I cannot conceive of his as any but a concrete immortality. If he lives, he lives as I knew
him and clothed as I knew him and with his unalterable voice, in a heaven of dædal flowers or a hell of
ineffectual flame; he lives, dreaming and talking and
explaining, explaining it all very earnestly and pre-
posterously, so I picture him, into the ear of the
amused, incredulous principal person in the place.

I have a real hatred for those dreary fools and
knaves who would have me suppose that Henley,
that crippled Titan, may conceivably be tapping at
the underside of a mahogany table or scratching
stifled incoherence into a locked slate ! Henley tapping !—for the professional purposes of Sludge ! If
he found himself among the circumstances of a spirit-
ualist séance he would, I know, instantly smash the
table with that big fist of his. And as the splinters
flew, surely York Powell, out of the dead past from
which he shines on me, would laugh that hearty
laugh of his back into the world again.

Henley is nowhere now except that, red-faced and
jolly like an October sunset, he leans over a gate at
Worthing after a long day of picnicking at Chancton-
bury Ring, or sits at his Woking table praising and
quoting *The Admirable Bashville*, or blue-shirted
and wearing the hat that Nicholson has painted, is
thrust and lugged, laughing and talking aside in his
bath-chair, along the Worthing esplanade. . . .

And Bob Stevenson walks for ever about a garden
in Chiswick, talking in the dusk.

§ 5

THE CONSOLATION OF FAILURE

That parable of the talents I have made such free use of in this book has one significant defect. It gives but two cases, and three are possible. There was first the man who buried his talent, and of his condemnation we are assured. But those others all took their talents and used them courageously and came back with gain. Was that gain inevitable? Does courage always ensure us victory? because if that is so we can all be heroes and valour is the better part of discretion. Alas! the faith in such magic dies. What of the possible case of the man who took his two or three talents and invested them as best he could and was deceived or heedless and lost them, interest and principal together?

There is something harder to face than death, and that is the realization of failure and misdirected effort and wrong-doing. Faith is no Open Sesame to right-doing, much less is it the secret of success. The service of God on earth is no processional triumph. What if one does wrong so extremely as to condemn one's life, to make oneself part of the refuse and not of the building? Or what if one is misjudged, or it may be too pitilessly judged, and one's co-operation despised and the help one brought becomes a source of weakness? Or suppose that the fine scheme one made lies shattered or wrecked by one's own act, or through some hidden blemish one's offering is rejected and flung back and one is thrust out?

So in the end it may be you or I will find we have been anvil and not hammer in the Purpose of God.

Then indeed will come the time for Faith, for the last word of Faith, to say still steadfastly, disgraced or dying, defeated or discredited, that all is well :—

" This and not that was my appointed work, and this I had to be."

§ 6

THE LAST CONFESSION

So these broken confessions and statements of mood and attitude come to an end.

But at this end, since I have, I perceive, run a little into a pietistic strain, I must repeat again how provisional and personal I know all these things to be. I began by disavowing ultimates. My beliefs, my dogmas, my rules, they are made for my campaigning needs, like the knapsack and water-bottle of a Cockney soldier invading some stupendous mountain gorge. About him are fastnesses and splendours, torrents and cataracts, glaciers and untrodden snows. He comes tramping on heel-worn boots and ragged socks. Beauties and blue mysteries shine upon him and appeal to him, the enigma of beauty smiling the faint strange smile of Leonardo's Mona Lisa. He sees a light on the grass like music ; and the blossom on the trees against the sky brings him near weeping. Such things come to him, give themselves to him. I do not know why he should not in response fling his shabby gear aside and behave like a god ; I only know that he does not do so. His grunt of appreciation is absurd, his speech goes like a crippled thing—and withal, and partly by virtue of the knapsack and water-bottle, he is conqueror of the valley. The valley is his for the taking.

There is a duality in life that I cannot express except by such images as this, a duality so that we are at once absurd and full of sublimity, and most absurd when we are most anxious to render the real splendours that pervade us. This duplicity in life seems to me at times ineradicable, at times like the confusing of something essentially simple, like the duplication when one looks through a doubly refracting medium. You think in this latter mood that you have only to turn the crystal of Iceland spar about in order to have the whole thing plain. But you never get it plain. I have been doing my halting utmost to set down sincerely and simply my vision of life and duty. I have permitted myself no defensive restraints ; I have shamelessly written my starkest, and it is plain to me that a smile that is not mine plays over my most urgent passages. There is a rebellious rippling of the grotesque under our utmost tragedy and gravity. One's martialled phrases grimace as one turns, and wink at the reader. None the less they signify. Do you note how in this that I have written, such a word as Believer will begin to wear a capital letter and give itself solemn ridiculous airs ? It does not matter. It carries its message for all that necessary superficial absurdity.

Thought has made me shameless. It does not matter at last at all if one is a little harsh or indelicate or ridiculous if that also is in the mystery of things.

Behind everything I perceive the smile that makes all effort and discipline temporary, all the stress and pain of life endurable. In the last resort I do not care whether I am seated on a throne or drunk or dying in a gutter. I follow my leading. I am more than myself, for I myself am Man. In the ultimate I know, though I cannot prove my knowledge in any way whatever, that everything is right and all things mine.

FAMOUS 2/6 CLASSICS

NET

POCKET EDITIONS

336 pp.; clothette, 2s. 6d. net, by post 2s. 10d.

HISTORY OF THE CONFLICT BETWEEN RELIGION AND SCIENCE

By JOHN WILLIAM DRAPER

DR. DRAPER, writing as an impartial student of history qualified to speak with authority on behalf of science, presents with fascinating skill the story of the " conflict of two contending powers—the expansive force of the human intellect on the one side and the compression arising from traditionary faith and human interests on the other." This book is for every reader who brings to the problems of history a desire to know the truth about them.

512 pp.; leather, 4s. 6d. net, by post 4s. 10d.; cloth, 2s. 6d. net, by post 2s. 10d.

THE MARTYRDOM OF MAN

By WINWOOD READE

MR. H. G. WELLS, in *The Outline of History*, thus writes of this famous historical masterpiece: " Remarkably few sketches of universal history by one single author have been written. One book that has influenced me very strongly is Winwood Reade's *Martyrdom of Man*. This ' DATES,' as people say nowadays, and it has a fine gloom of its own ; but it is still an extraordinarily inspiring presentation of human history as one consistent process."

ALSO

TWELVE YEARS IN A MONASTERY,
by JOSEPH McCABE

SELECTED PROSE WORKS OF SHELLEY

London : WATTS & CO., Johnson's Court, Fleet Street, E.C.4

THE FORUM SERIES

Each volume bound in clothette at 1s. net (by post 1s. 2d.),
and in paper cover at 7d. net (by post 8d.).

THE STREAM OF LIFE.
By Professor JULIAN S. HUXLEY.

Manchester Guardian.—" It would be hard to find a better or more stimulating introduction to the general study of biology."

THE RELIGION OF AN ARTIST.
By the Hon. JOHN COLLIER

Nation and Athenæum.—" It could hardly be improved."

MR. BELLOC OBJECTS TO " THE OUTLINE OF HISTORY."
By H. G. WELLS.

An acute and masterly criticism.

THE GOODNESS OF GODS.
By EDWARD WESTERMARCK, Ph.D.

Dr. Westermarck wields a facile pen, and he has never used it to greater effect than he has done in this delightful work.

CONCERNING MAN'S ORIGIN.
By Prof. Sir ARTHUR KEITH.

The Presidential Address to the British Association, 1927 (with additions), and other Essays.

THE EARTH : ITS NATURE AND HISTORY.
By EDWARD GREENLY, D.Sc., F.G.S.

Sheffield Daily Telegraph.—" For the beginner in the science of geology it is one of the most useful books yet published."

CRAFTSMANSHIP AND SCIENCE.
By Prof. WILLIAM H. BRAGG.

The Presidential Address to the British Association, 1928, with supplementary Essays.

DARWINISM AND WHAT IT IMPLIES.
By Prof. Sir ARTHUR KEITH.

Contains the famous Ludwig Mond lecture, dealing with Immortality.

WHAT IS EUGENICS ?
By Major LEONARD DARWIN.

A comprehensive exposition, including a chapter on Birth Control.

THE MEANING OF LIFE, AS SHOWN IN THE PROCESS OF EVOLUTION.
By C. E. M. JOAD.

A subtle and powerful exposition of Vitalism.

London : WATTS & CO., Johnson's Court, Fleet Street, E.C.4